SIGN REFERENCE
(signs used in the ~~~~; ams)

Good footpath ~~~~~
(sufficiently distinct ~~~~~ followed in mist)

Intermittent footpath ~~~~~
(difficult to follow in mist)

Route recommended
   but no path
(if recommended one way only, arrow indicates direction)

Wall ∞∞∞∞∞∞∞∞∞   **Broken wall** •••••••••••••••••

Fence ++++++++++++   **Broken fence** ''''''''''''''''''''

Marshy ground ¼¼¼¼   **Trees** ꙮꙮꙮꙮ

Crags ⚞⚟⚞⚟   **Boulders** ∘∘∘∘∘

Stream or River ～～～～～→
   (arrow indicates direction of flow)

Waterfall ⌇⌇⌇   **Bridge** ～⨯～

Buildings ▪▪▪   **Unenclosed road** ‥‥‥‥‥

Contours (at 100' intervals) ⋯⋯⋯ _1900_ _1800_ _1700_

Summit-cairn ▲   **Other** (prominent) **cairns** △

THE
EASTERN
FELLS

A PICTORIAL GUIDE
TO THE
LAKELAND FELLS

being an illustrated account
of a study and exploration
of the mountains in the
English Lake District

by

A Wainwright

BOOK ONE
THE EASTERN FELLS

MICHAEL JOSEPH LTD

Published by the Penguin Group
27 Wrights Lane, London W8, England

Penguin Books Ltd Registered Offices:
Harmondsworth, Middlesex, England

First published by Michael Joseph
1992
Originally published by the Westmorland Gazette, 1955

Printed by Titus Wilson and Son, Kendal

ISBN 0 7181 4000 1

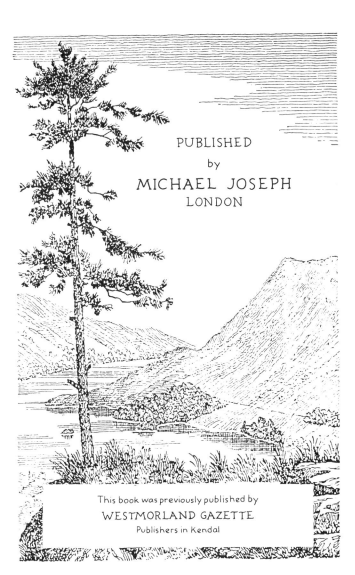

PUBLISHED
by
MICHAEL JOSEPH
LONDON

This book was previously published by
WESTMORLAND GAZETTE
Publishers in Kendal

Publisher's Note

This book is a re-issue of the original volume written by A. Wainwright. The descriptions of the walks were correct, to the best of A. Wainwright's knowledge, at the time of first publication and are reproduced here without amendment at the wish of the Wainwright Estate. However, since certain footpaths, cairns and other waymarks described here may no longer be accurate, walkers are advised to check with an up-to-date Ordnance Survey map when planning a walk.

BOOK ONE

is dedicated to

THE MEN OF THE ORDNANCE SURVEY

whose maps of Lakeland
have given me much pleasure
both on the fells
and by my fireside

INTRODUCTION

Surely there is no other place in this whole wonderful world quite like Lakeland ...no other so exquisitely lovely, no other so charming, no other that calls so insistently across a gulf of distance. All who truly love Lakeland are exiles when away from it.

Here, in small space, is the wonderland of childhood's dreams, lingering far beyond childhood through the span of a man's life: its enchantment grows with passing years and quiet eventide is enriched by the haunting sweetness of dear memories, memories that remain evergreen through the flight of time, that refresh and sustain in the darker days. How many, these memories........... the moment of wakening, and the sudden joyful realisation that this is to be another day of freedom on the hills........ the dawn chorus of bird-song........ the delicate lacework of birches against the sky ...... morning sun drawing aside the veils of mist; black-stockinged lambs, in springtime, amongst the daffodils......... silver cascades dancing and leaping down bracken steeps..... autumn colours ....a red fox running over snow .... the silence of lonely hills...... storm and tempest in the high places, and the unexpected glimpses of valleys dappled in sunlight far beneath the swirling clouds............. rain, and the intimate shelter of lichened walls......... fierce winds on the heights and soft breezes that are no more than gentle caresses..........a sheepdog watching its master

.... the snow and ice and freezing stillnesses of midwinter: a white world, rosy-pink as the sun goes down .... the supreme moment when the top cairn comes into sight at last, only minutes away, after the long climb .... the small ragged sheep that brave the blizzards .... the symphonies of murmuring streams, unending, with never a discord .... curling smoke from the chimneys of the farm down below amongst the trees, where the day shall end ...... oil-lamps in flagged kitchens, huge fires in huge fireplaces, huge suppers .... glittering moonlight on placid waters ...... stars above dark peaks ..... the tranquillity that comes before sleep, when thoughts are of the day that is gone and the day that is to come .... All these memories, and so many more, breathing anew the rare quality and magical atmosphere of Lakeland .... memories that belong to Lakeland, and could not belong in the same way to any other place .... memories that enslave the mind forever.

Many are they who have fallen under the spell of Lakeland, and many are they who have been moved to tell of their affection, in story and verse and picture and song.

This book is one man's way of expressing his devotion to Lakeland's friendly hills. It was conceived, and is born, after many years of inarticulate worshipping at their shrines.

It is, in very truth, a love-letter.

INTRODUCTION

Classification and Definition

Any division of the Lakeland fells into geographical districts must necessarily be arbitrary, just as the location of the outer boundaries of Lakeland must always be a matter of opinion. Any attempt to define internal or external boundaries is certain to invite criticism, and he who takes it upon himself to say where Lakeland starts and finishes, or, for example, where the Central Fells merge into the Southern Fells and *which* fells are the Central Fells and which the Southern and *why* they need be so classified, must not expect his pronouncements to be generally accepted.

Yet for present purposes some plan of classification and definition must be used. County and parochial boundaries are no help, nor is the recently-defined area of the Lakeland National Park, for this book is concerned only with the high ground.

First, the external boundaries. Straight lines linking the extremities of the outlying lakes enclose all the higher fells very conveniently. There are a few fells of lesser height to the north and east, however, that are typically Lakeland in character and cannot properly be omitted : these are brought in, somewhat untidily, by extending the lines in those areas. Thus:

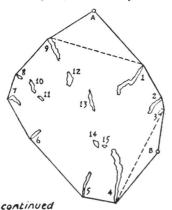

1 : *Ullswater*
2 : *Hawes Water*
3 : proposed *Swindale Rest*
4 : *Windermere*
5 : *Coniston Water*
6 : *Wast Water*
7 : *Ennerdale Water*
8 : *Loweswater*
9 : *Bassenthwaite Lake*
10 : *Crummock Water*
11 : *Buttermere*
12 : *Derwent Water*
13 : *Thirlmere*
14 : *Grasmere*
15 : *Rydal Water*
A : *Caldbeck*
B : *Longsleddale (church)*

continued

Classification and Definition

continued   The complete Guide is planned to include all the fells in the area enclosed by the straight lines of the diagram. This is an undertaking quite beyond the compass of a single volume, and it is necessary, therefore, to divide the area into convenient sections, making the fullest use of natural boundaries (lakes, valleys and low passes) so that each district is, as far as possible, self-contained and independent of the rest.

This division gives seven areas, each with a well-defined group of fells, and each will be the subject of a separate volume

1 : The Eastern Fells
2 : The Far Eastern Fells
3 : The Central Fells
4 : The Southern Fells
5 : The Northern Fells
6 : The North-western Fells
7 : The Western Fells

INTRODUCTION

Notes on the *Illustrations*

THE MAPS.................Many excellent books have been written about Lakeland, but the best literature of all for the walker is that published by the Director General of Ordnance Survey, the 1" map for companionship and guidance on expeditions, the 2½" map for exploration both on the fells and by the fireside. These admirable maps are remarkably accurate topographically but there is a crying need for a revision of the paths on the hills: several walkers' tracks that have come into use during the past few decades, some of them now broad highways, are not shown at all; other paths still shown on the maps have fallen into neglect and can no longer be traced on the ground.

The popular Bartholomew 1" map is a beautiful picture, fit for a frame, but this too is unreliable for paths; indeed here the defect is much more serious, for routes are indicated where no paths ever existed, nor ever could — the cartographer has preferred to take precipices in his stride rather than deflect his graceful curves over easy ground.

Hence the justification for the maps in this book: they have the one merit (of importance to walkers) of being dependable as regards delineation of *paths*. They are intended as supplements to the Ordnance Survey maps, certainly not as substitutes.

THE VIEWS...............Various devices have been used to illustrate the views from the summits of the fells. The full panorama in the form of an outline drawing is most satisfactory generally, and this method has been adopted for the main viewpoints.

THE DIAGRAMS OF ASCENTS...................The routes of ascent of the higher fells are depicted by diagrams that do not pretend to strict accuracy: they are neither plans nor elevations; in fact there is deliberate distortion in order to show detail clearly: usually they are represented as viewed from imaginary 'space-stations.' But it is hoped they will be useful and interesting.

THE DRAWINGS.......The drawings at least are honest attempts to reproduce what the eye sees: they illustrate features of interest and also serve the dual purpose of breaking up the text and balancing the layout of the pages, and of filling up awkward blank spaces, like this:

Thirlmere

THE
EASTERN
FELLS

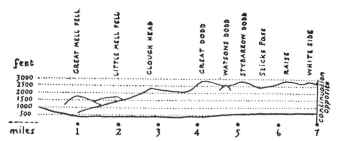

In the area of the Eastern Fells the greatest single mass of high ground in Lakeland is concentrated. It takes the form of a tremendous barrier running north and south, consistently high and steep throughout its length, mainly having an altitude between 2500'-3000', in two places only falling below 2000', and rising above 3000' on Helvellyn. In general the western slopes are steep, smooth and grassy and the eastern slopes are broken and craggy, but at the northern extremity the reverse obtains. The fells in this area may conveniently be classed in two groups divided by Grisedale Pass: in the south is the Fairfield group, pleasingly arrayed and with deep valleys cutting into the mass on both flanks; north is the bigger but less interesting Helvellyn range, with no valleys in the high western wall but several on the eastern side running down to Ullswater.

The geographical boundaries of the area are distinct. In shape it is a long inverted triangle, covering about fifty square miles of territory, based on Ambleside. The western boundary is formed by the deep trough of Dunmail Raise and Thirlmere, a great rift of which the principal road across the district takes advantage;

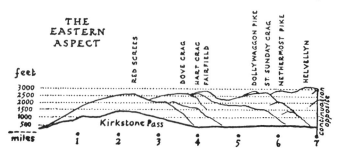

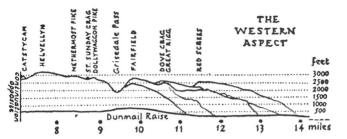

THE
WESTERN
ASPECT

CATSTYCAM
HELVELLYN
NETHERMOST PIKE
ST. SUNDAY CRAG / DOLLYWAGGON PIKE
Grisedale Pass
FAIRFIELD
DOVE CRAG / GREAT RIGG
RED SCREES

feet
3000
2500
2000
1500
1000
500

continuation opposite

Dunmail Raise

8   9   10   11   12   13   14 miles

the eastern boundary is the trench of Kirkstone Pass
and Ullswater, and the northern is the broad Keswick
to Penrith gap. These boundaries are very satisfactory,
enclosing all the dependencies of Helvellyn and Fairfield,
and they are particularly convenient for the purposes
of a separate guidebook because they are not crossed,
normally, during the course of a day's fell-walk. Only
at Kirkstone is there a link with fells outside the area
but even here the breach is very pronounced.

This is an area easily accessible and (excepting the fells
north of Sticks Pass) much frequented by walkers. It has
in Helvellyn the most-often-climbed mountain in Lakeland
and in Grisedale Pass one of the best-known footpaths.

Ambleside and Grasmere are favourite resorts for those
who frequent these fells, but, because the most dramatic
features are invariably presented to the east, the quiet
and beautiful Patterdale valley is far superior as a base
for their exploration: the eastern approaches are more
interesting, the surroundings more charming and the
views more rewarding; furthermore, from Patterdale
any part of the main ridge may be visited in a normal
day's expedition.

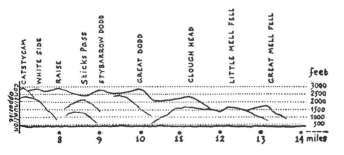

CATSTYCAM
WHITE SIDE
RAISE
Sticks Pass
STYBARROW DODD
GREAT DODD
CLOUGH HEAD
LITTLE MELL FELL
GREAT MELL FELL

feet
3000
2500
2000
1500
1000
500

continuation opposite

8   9   10   11   12   13   14 miles

THE EASTERN FELLS

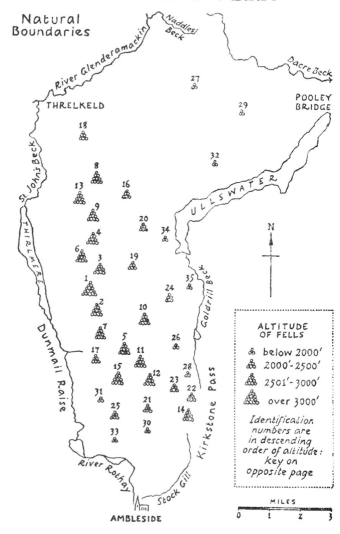

Natural
Boundaries

Naddles Beck

River Glenderamackin

Dacre Beck

THRELKELD

POOLEY
BRIDGE

27

29

St. John's Beck

18

32

8

13   16

ULLSWATER

9

20

THIRLMERE

4   34

N

6   3   19

35

1   24

Goldrill Beck

2   10

7

26

5

17   11

15

28

12   23

31   21   22

25   14

30

Kirkstone Pass

33

Dunmail Raise

ALTITUDE
OF FELLS

🔺 below 2000'
🔺 2000'–2500'
🔺 2501'–3000'
🔺 over 3000'

*Identification
numbers are
in descending
order of altitude:
key on
opposite page*

River Rothay

Stock Gill

AMBLESIDE

MILES

0   1   2   3

THE EASTERN FELLS

in the order of their appearance in this book

Each fell is the subject of a separate chapter

Arnison Crag

from Keldas

Glenridding

Patterdale

ARNISON CRAG

BIRKS ▲

ST SUNDAY CRAG
▲

MILES

0   1   2

The rough fellside curving out of Deepdale and bounding the highway to Patterdale village has an attractive rocky crown, often visited for the fine view it offers of the head of Ullswater. This is Arnison Crag, a low hill with a summit worthy of a mountain. It is a dependency of St Sunday Crag, forming the lesser of the two prongs which constitute the north-east spur of that grand fell; Birks is the other. It starts as a grass shelf east of Cold Cove and then takes the shape of a curving ridge of no particular interest except for the sudden upthrust of its craggy summit.

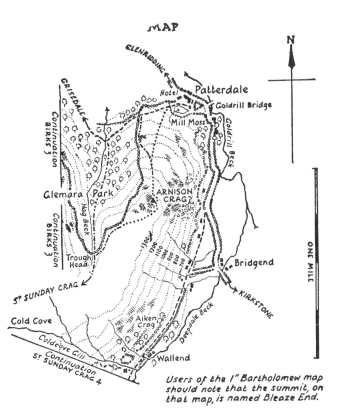

MAP

Users of the 1" Bartholomew map should note that the summit, on that map, is named Bleaze End.

ASCENT FROM PATTERDALE

The ascent is invariably made from the village of Patterdale. Behind the cluster of buildings is Mill Moss (once a pleasant tarn, now a refuse tip) and, after picking a way through the foothills of old tin cans and motor tyres which are much in evidence here, the climb may be started from the wire fence, inclining right to the ridge. In summer, however, high bracken hinders progress and it is easier to keep to the path as far as the wall enclosing Glemara Park and then follow the wall up, slanting across to the ridge above the first crag. The summit is finally attained after a steep scramble. *Although a short and easy walk, the ascent may lead to difficulties in mist and should then not be attempted.*

THE SUMMIT

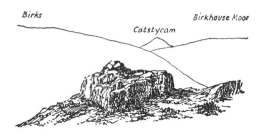

The summit is a rock platform, inaccessible to the walker on the west side and attained from other directions only by breaches in a low wall of crag defending it. A rock gateway (seen from the road near Hartsop as a clean-cut notch on the skyline) separates this platform from another at a slightly lower elevation which has the principal cairn and overlooks the approach from Patterdale.

The lower cairn

The summit from the south

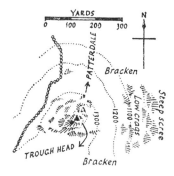

DESCENTS: The ridge should be followed down, for Patterdale. 'Short cuts' are likely to encounter rougher ground. A longer alternative follows the wall to Trough Head, where a very awkward stepstile gives access to the wooded Glemara Park and pleasant paths which lead back to Patterdale — pleasant, at any rate, until arrival at the environs of Mill Moss.

‖ *In mist*, make a wide detour to the ‖ wall and follow it down northwards.

THE VIEW

Arnison Crag is surrounded by higher fells, and the view is very restricted. A feature is the fine grouping of the hills above the pastures of Hartsop.

Ullswater is the only lake seen, its upper reach being well displayed. This is not, however, the best viewpoint for Ullswater by any means.

Principal Fells

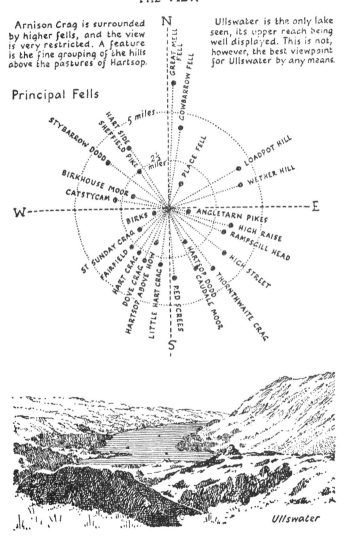

Ullswater

Birkhouse Moor

2350' approx.

RAISE
Glenridding
BIRKHOUSE MOOR
Patterdale
HELVELLYN
▲ FAIRFIELD

MILES
0 1 2 3 4

from Lanty's Tarn

NATURAL FEATURES

The east ridge of Helvellyn starts as a narrow rock arete, known to all walkers as Striding Edge, and then gradually widens into the broad sprawling mass of Birkhouse Moor. A long grassy promenade is the main characteristic of the top, but the southern slopes soon steepen to form a natural wall for Grisedale for two miles; this flank is traversed by one of the most popular paths in the district. Northwards, Red Tarn Beck and Glenridding Beck form its boundaries; there are crags on this side, mainly concentrated around the only defined ridge descending from the summit, north-east. The name 'moor' is well suited to this fell, the top particularly being grassy and dull; below, eastwards, there are patches of heather, and in this direction the fell ends abruptly and craggily above Ullswater, the lower slopes being beautifully wooded.

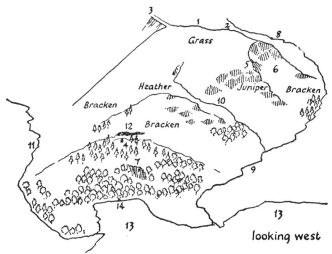

looking west

1: The highest point	8: Red Tarn Beck
2: The cairn at 2318'	9: Glenridding Beck
3: Ridge continuing to Helvellyn	10: Mires Beck
4: Keldas	11: Grisedale Beck
5: The north-east ridge	12: Lanty's Tarn
6: Blea Cove	13: Ullswater
7: Raven Crag	14: St. Patrick's Well

MAP

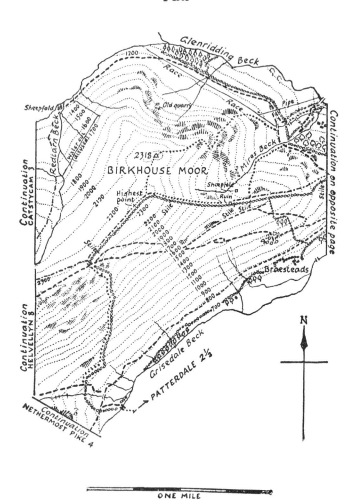

ONE MILE

MAP

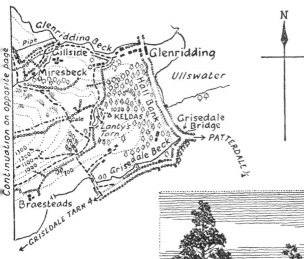

Continuation on opposite page

KELDAS ——

Birkhouse Moor falls away to the east in bracken-clad slopes, but its extremity is an abrupt wooded height overlooking the upper reach of Ullswater. This height has no name on official maps; locally it is referred to as Keldas. The pines here are a joy to behold, framing very beautiful views of the nearby lake and fells. The cairn on its summit is accessible from Lanty's Tarn, but the eastern face is very steep and craggy. Artists and photographers will vote Keldas the loveliest and most delightful place amongst the eastern fells.

Ullswater from Keldas

ASCENT FROM GRISEDALE
1900 feet of ascent : 3½ miles from Patterdale village

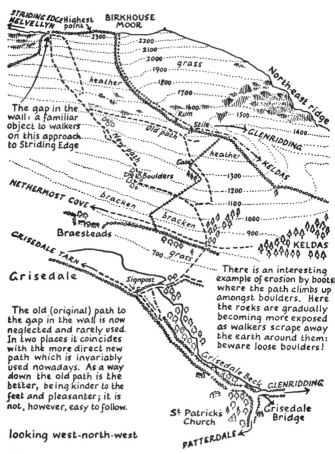

STRIDING EDGE
HELVELLYN Highest point   BIRKHOUSE MOOR

2300
2200
2100
2000
1900 grass
1800
heather   1700
1600
Rum   1500
Old path   Stile   GLENRIDDING
1400
KELDAS
heather
1300
Gate
Boulders   1200
1100
New path
NETHERMOST COVE   bracken   1000
900
bracken
Braesteads   700 grass   KELDAS
GRISEDALE TARN

Grisedale

Signpost

Grisedale Beck   GLENRIDDING
St Patrick's Church   Grisedale Bridge
PATTERDALE

North-east ridge

The gap in the wall: a familiar object to walkers on this approach to Striding Edge

The old (original) path to the gap in the wall is now neglected and rarely used. In two places it coincides with the more direct new path which is invariably used nowadays. As a way down the old path is the better, being kinder to the feet and pleasanter; it is not, however, easy to follow.

looking west-north-west

There is an interesting example of erosion by boots where the path climbs up amongst boulders. Here the rocks are gradually becoming more exposed as walkers scrape away the earth around them: beware loose boulders!

Birkhouse Moor may most easily be ascended by using the well-defined Patterdale-Striding Edge path climbing across its flank. The splendid views of Grisedale are the chief merit of this route, which is safe in bad conditions.

ASCENT FROM GLENRIDDING
1900 feet of ascent : 2 miles

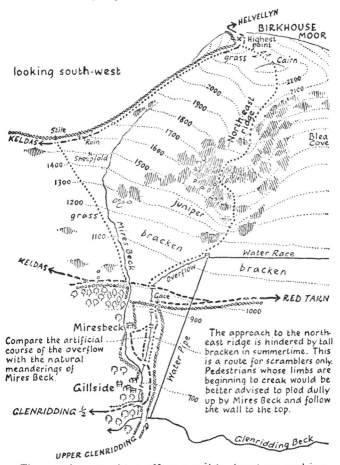

looking south-west

HELVELLYN
BIRKHOUSE MOOR
Highest point
grass
Cairn
Stile
KELDAS
Ruin
Blea Cove
Sheepfold
Northeast ridge
1400
1300
1200
grass
Mires Beck
juniper
bracken
1100
2000
1900
1800
1700
1600
1500
2200
2100
KELDAS
Water Race
bracken
Overflow
Gate
RED TARN
Miresbeck
900
1000
Compare the artificial course of the overflow with the natural meanderings of Mires Beck.

The approach to the north-east ridge is hindered by tall bracken in summertime. This is a route for scramblers only. Pedestrians whose limbs are beginning to creak would be better advised to plod dully up by Mires Beck and follow the wall to the top.

Gillside
Water Pipe
GLENRIDDING ½
700
UPPER GLENRIDDING
Glenridding Beck

The north-east ridge offers a mild adventure and is a test in route-finding amongst low crags. It is the best way up, with a beautiful view in retrospect, but in bad weather the Mires Beck route is preferable, and safer.

THE SUMMIT

Helvellyn

Striding Edge

The highest point

The cairn at 2318'

The top can be reached easily and quickly from the popular Striding Edge path, but the detour is not really worth making. A few small tarns relieve the monotony of the grassy expanse, but generally the summit is without interest. A cairn indicates what appears to be the natural summit, but the prominent wall actually passes over higher ground.

2318 → North-east ridge

N

Small tarns

Grass

PATTERDALE and GLENRIDDING →

Highest point x

HELVELLYN ← 2700 2200 2100 2000

YARDS

0   100   200   300

The summit of Keldas

DESCENTS: The descent is best made by following the wall east to the saddle above Mires Beck: here turn left for Glenridding, or (for Patterdale) cross the wall at the stile to join a path going down to the right. The north-east ridge is not suitable for descent.

In bad weather conditions follow the wall east as far as Keldas. Avoid the east and north faces.

THE VIEW

The east face of Helvellyn, enclosed between the twin arms of Striding Edge and Swirral Edge, is the best feature of a rather dull panorama.

Lakes and Tarns
N: Sticks Res'r
NE: Ullswater
(better seen from the cairn at 2318)
ESE: Angle Tarn
SE: Hayes Water
S: Grisedale Tarn
WNW: Keppelcove Tarn (dry)

Principal Fells
(from the highest point)

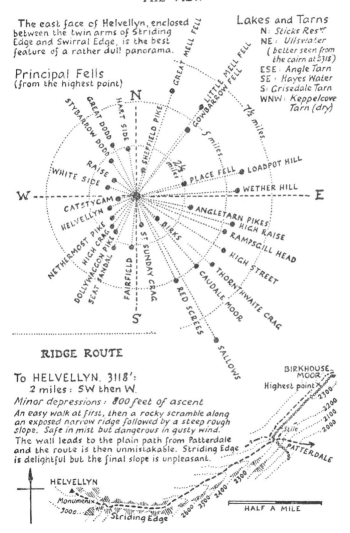

RIDGE ROUTE

To HELVELLYN, 3118':
2 miles : SW then W.

Minor depressions : 800 feet of ascent

An easy walk at first, then a rocky scramble along an exposed narrow ridge followed by a steep rough slope. Safe in mist but dangerous in gusty wind. The wall leads to the plain path from Patterdale and the route is then unmistakable. Striding Edge is delightful but the final slope is unpleasant.

HALF A MILE

Birks

from Ullswater

Glenridding

Patterdale

ARNISON CRAG ▲

BIRKS ▲

St SUNDAY CRAG
▲

MILES
0   1   2

The north-east shoulder of St Sunday Crag falls sharply to a depression beyond which a grassy undulating spur, featureless and wide, continues with little change in elevation towards Ullswater before finally plunging down to the valley through the enclosure of Glemara Park. Although this spur lacks a distinctive summit it is sufficiently well-defined to deserve a separate name; but, being an unromantic and uninteresting fell, it has earned for itself nothing better than the prosaic and unassuming title of Birks. It is rarely visited as the sole objective of an expedition, but walkers descending the ridge from St Sunday Crag often take it in their stride.

NATURAL FEATURES

Above the 1900' contour Birks is a half-mile's easy grass promenade and there is nothing here to suggest that there are formidable crags below on both sides. Yet the Grisedale flank has a continuous line of cliffs and round to the east are several tiers of rock above the lower wooded slopes of Glemara Park. Beyond the hollow of Trough Head, where rises Birks' only stream of note, is a curving ridge which culminates in the rocky pyramid of Arnison Crag; both his lower ridge and Birks itself, together forming a high wedge of rough ground between Grisedale and Deepdale, are dependencies of St Sunday Crag, Birks especially being dominated by this fine mountain.

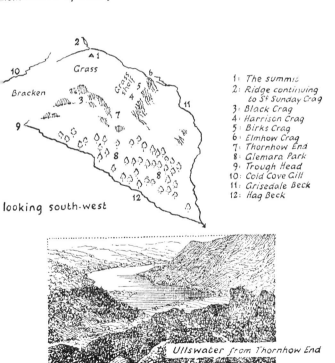

looking south-west

1: The summit
2: Ridge continuing to St Sunday Crag
3: Black Crag
4: Harrison Crag
5: Birks Crag
6: Elmhow Crag
7: Thornhow End
8: Glemara Park
9: Trough Head
10: Cold Cove Gill
11: Grisedale Beck
12: Hag Beck

Ullswater from Thornhow End

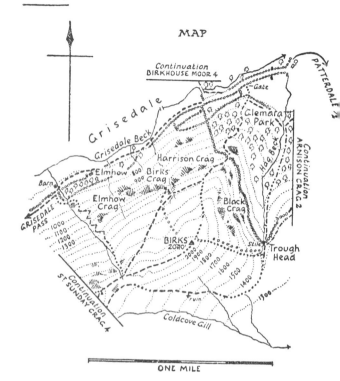

MAP

Continuation
BIRKHOUSE MOOR 4

PATTERDALE 2

Grisedale

Glemara
Park

Grisedale Beck

Gate

Harrison Crag

Hag Beck

Elmhow

Birks
Crag

Continuation
ARNISON CRAG 2

Barn

Elmhow
Crag

800
900

Black
Crag

GRISEDALE
PASS

1000
1100
1200
1300

BIRKS
2040

2000
1900
1800
1700
1600
1500
1400

Stile

Trough
Head

Continuation
ST SUNDAY CRAG 4

Ruin

1900

Coldcove Gill

ONE MILE

Place Fell from Glemara Park

ASCENTS FROM PATTERDALE
1600 feet of ascent · 2½ miles (1¾ by short variations)

by Trough Head

looking west-south-west

ST SUNDAY CRAG

Col

Path in groove

Ruin ×

bracken

BIRKS

2000 grass
1900
1800
1700
1600
1500
1400 Awkward
1300 stile

Black Crag

Thornhow End

Trough Head

Hag Beck

1200

1100

Glemara Park

There used to be a good track between Trough Head and the col but the beginning and the end of it have now vanished and the middle is difficult to find. Much time will be saved by following the broken wall directly up the fell from Trough Head.

Mill Moss

Patterdale

by Thornhow End

BIRKS

ST SUNDAY CRAG

Col

Black Crag

grass

2000
1900
1800
1700

Rock-shelter

1400

Thornhow End

1300

1200

1100

Glemara Park

PATTERDALE (footpath) ½

Gates

PATTERDALE ¾

GRISEDALE PASS →

Grisedale Beck

Above the wall on Thornhow End the path ascends in a groove to a grass shelf. The summit-ridge may be reached from the top of the groove by inclining left.
On the fellside above the groove there is a small natural rock-shelter at the foot of a low crag, identifiable by two rowans growing from it.

looking south-south-west

The Thornhow End path is very attractive, with glorious views, but it is steep. The Trough Head route is without a path in places and is uninteresting. There is no pleasure, and some danger, in climbing Birks in misty conditions.

THE SUMMIT

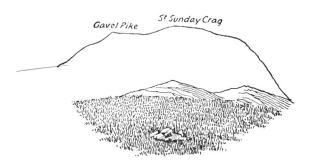

The summit has no interesting features. The Ordnance Survey one-inch map promises a beacon on the highest point, but all that can be found is an insignificant mound of stones almost obscured by grass. A more considerable heap of bigger stones further along the ridge appears to be a collapsed edifice of some kind.

There is a narrow track along the crest but none on the actual summit.

DESCENTS: The finest way down (because of the view of Ullswater) is by the ridge to the north, inclining left to the path on the grass shelf below to avoid steep rough ground at the end of the ridge.

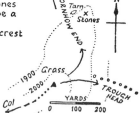

In bad weather conditions, search eastwards for the top of the broken wall and follow it down to Trough Head.

RIDGE ROUTE

To ST SUNDAY CRAG
2756' : 1¼ miles : SW
Minor depressions
800 feet of ascent

An easy stroll on grass to the col is followed by steep climbing up the ridge to the sloping summit-plateau; the alternative path (left) is easier. Not recommended in mist.

THE VIEW

This is a scene of strong contrasts, interesting and pleasing but not extensive.

Principal Fells

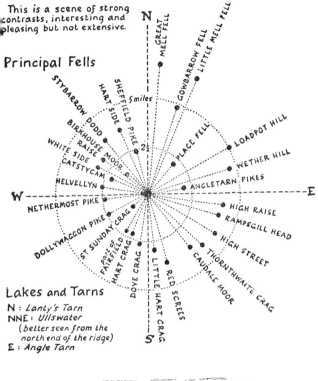

Lakes and Tarns

N : *Lanty's Tarn*
NNE : *Ullswater*
  (better seen from the
  north end of the ridge)
E : *Angle Tarn*

Ullswater

Catstycam

2917′

sometimes called
Catchedicam

from Glenridding Beck

RAISE
Glenridding

CATSTYCAM
Patterdale

HELVELLYN

MILES
0   1   2   3   4

NATURAL FEATURES

If Catstycam stood alone, remote from its fellows, it would be one of the finest peaks in Lakeland. It has nearly, but not quite, the perfect mountain form, with true simplicity in its soaring lines, and a small pointed top, a real summit, that falls away sharply on all sides. From Birkhouse Moor especially it has the appearance of a symmetrical pyramid; and from the upper valley of Glenridding it towers into the sky most impressively. But when seen from other directions it is too obviously dominated by Helvellyn and although its sharp peaked top identifies it unmistakably in every view in which it appears, clearly it is no more than the abrupt terminus of a short spur of the higher mountain, to which it is connected by a fine rock ridge, Swirral Edge. Its best feature is the tremendous shattered face it presents to the valley to the north, riven by a great scree gully. The steep slopes are nearly dry, but there is marshy ground around the base; the waters from Catstycam drain into Red Tarn Beck and Glenridding Beck.

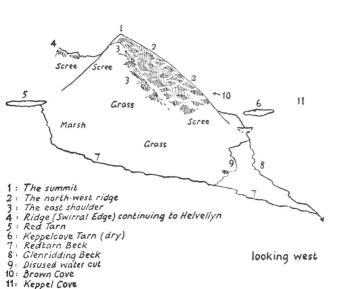

1: The summit
2: The north-west ridge
3: The east shoulder
4: Ridge (Swirral Edge) continuing to Helvellyn
5: Red Tarn
6: Keppelcove Tarn (dry)
7: Redtarn Beck
8: Glenridding Beck
9: Disused water cut
10: Brown Cove
11: Keppel Cove

looking west

MAP

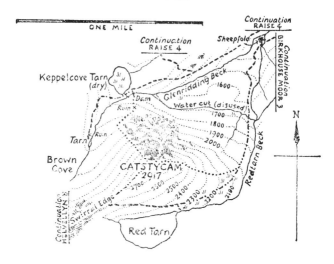

Helvellyn and Swirral Edge

ASCENT FROM GLENRIDDING
2500 feet of ascent : 4 miles from Glenridding village

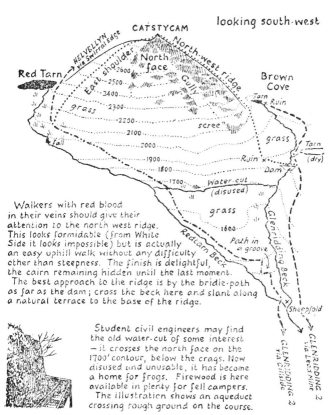

looking south-west

Walkers with red blood in their veins should give their attention to the north west ridge. This looks formidable (from White Side it looks impossible) but is actually an easy uphill walk without any difficulty other than steepness. The finish is delightful, the cairn remaining hidden until the last moment.

The best approach to the ridge is by the bridle-path as far as the dam; cross the beck here and slant along a natural terrace to the base of the ridge.

Student civil engineers may find the old water-cut of some interest — it crosses the north face on the 1700' contour, below the crags. Now disused and unusable, it has become a home for frogs. Firewood is here available in plenty for fell campers.

The illustration shows an aqueduct crossing rough ground on the course.

Of the two routes shown, that by Redtarn Beck and the east shoulder is easy, on grass all the way. The north-west ridge is steep and stony but a good airy climb in its later stages, giving a fine sense of achievement when the summit is gained. Catstycam should be avoided in bad weather.

THE SUMMIT

Sheffield Pike
Place Fell
Birkhouse Moor

Catstycam is a true peak, and its small shapely summit is the finest in the eastern fells; if it were rock and not mainly grass it would be the finest in the district. Here the highest point is not in doubt!

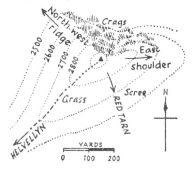

DESCENTS: The quickest and easiest descent is by the east shoulder to Glenridding. The north-west ridge is easy but too steep for comfort. For Patterdale, incline right from the east shoulder and cross Redtarn Beck high up, to join the Striding Edge path.

In bad conditions use the east shoulder, keeping right rather than left in mist, to Redtarn Beck and so down to Glenridding.

KEPPELCOVE TARN
AND ITS ENVIRONS
— a study in devastation

The burst banks

The breached dam

Keppelcove Tarn is now a marsh. Formerly it served as a reservoir for the Glenridding lead mine. In October 1927, following a cloudburst, flooded waters burst the banks of the tarn, carved out a new ravine, and caused great damage. The dam was breached later, in 1931, and has never been repaired.

The North-west Ridge, from White Side

THE VIEW

Catstycam, like all the satellites of Helvellyn, is robbed of a comprehensive view by Helvellyn itself, close at hand and higher. There is, however, an array of distant fells over the saddle between Helvellyn Lower Man and White Side. Eastwards the prospect is good.

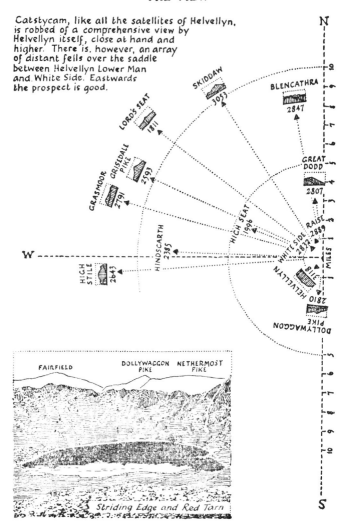

N

SKIDDAW
3053

BLENCATHRA
2847

LORDS SEAT
1811

GREAT DODD
2807

GRISEDALE PIKE
2593

GRASMOOR
2791

HIGH SEAT
1996

WHITE SIDE
2832

RAISE
2889

HINDSCARTH
2385

HELVELLYN
3118

W

HIGH STILE
2643

2810

DOLLYWAGGON PIKE

MILES

FAIRFIELD   DOLLYWAGGON PIKE   NETHERMOST PIKE

Striding Edge and Red Tarn

S

THE VIEW

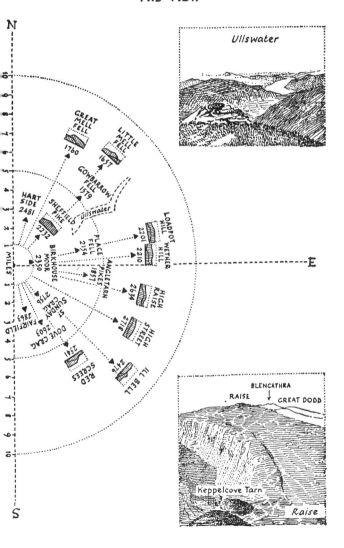

Ullswater

BLENCATHRA

RAISE   GREAT DODD

Keppelcove Tarn

Raise

from High Rigg

• Threlkeld

Wanthwaite
•
▲ CLOUGH
HEAD

▲ GREAT
DODD

• Legburthwaite
MILES
0   1   2   3

From Kirkstone Pass the massive main ridge of the Fairfield and Helvellyn fells runs north, mile after mile, throughout maintaining a consistently high and a remarkably uniform altitude, and with a dozen distinct summits over 2500'. At its northern extremity the ground falls away swiftly to the deep valley of the Glenderamackin, and the last outpost of the ridge, although not so elevated as the summits to the south, occupies a commanding site: this is Clough Head.

NATURAL FEATURES

Contrary to the usual pattern of the Helvellyn fells, of which it is the most northerly member, Clough Head displays its crags to the west and grassy slopes to the east. These crags form a steep, continuous, mile-long wall above St John's-in-the-Vale, with one breach only where a walker may safely venture; they are riven by deep gullies, one of which (Sandbed Gill) is the rockiest and roughest watercourse in the Helvellyn range. After initial steep scree, the northern slopes descend gently to the wide valley of the Glenderamackin at Threlkeld. Clough Head is an interesting fell, not only for walkers and explorers but for the ornithologist and botanist, the geologist and antiquarian also; while the merely curious traveller may content himself by puzzling out why and for what purpose Fisher's wife trod so persistently that remarkable path to Jim's Fold.

looking east

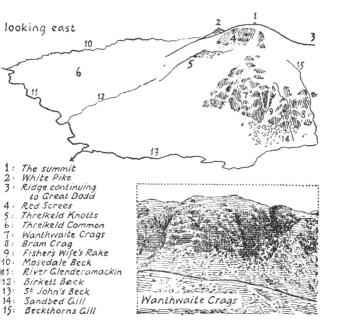

1 : The summit
2 : White Pike
3 : Ridge continuing to Great Dodd
4 : Red Screes
5 : Threlkeld Knotts
6 : Threlkeld Common
7 : Wanthwaite Crags
8 : Bram Crag
9 : Fisher's Wife's Rake
10 : Mosedale Beck
11 : River Glenderamackin
12 : Birkett Beck
13 : St John's Beck
14 : Sandbed Gill
15 : Beckthorns Gill

Wanthwaite Crags

MAP

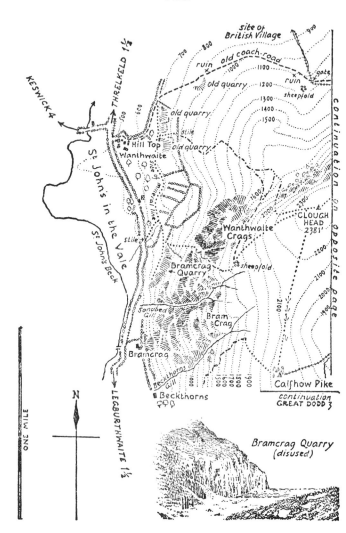

site of British Village

old coach-road

ruin

900

700 — 800

1000

1100

old quarry

1200

ruin

sheepfold

gate

1300

1400

1500

THRELKELD 1½

old quarry

600

stile

old quarry

KESWICK 4

500

Hill Top
Wanthwaite

1100

continuation on opposite page

St John's in the Vale

1200

CLOUGH HEAD
2381'

Wanthwaite
Crags

2200

St John's Beck

stile

2100

Bramcrag
Quarry

sheepfold

2000

1900

Scandbed Gill

Bram
Crag

2100

Bramcrag

1500

Beckthorns Gill

1600

1700

1800

900

Calfhow Pike

continuation
GREAT DODD 3

Beckthorns

N

ONE MILE

LEGBURTHWAITE 1½

Bramcrag Quarry
(disused)

MAP

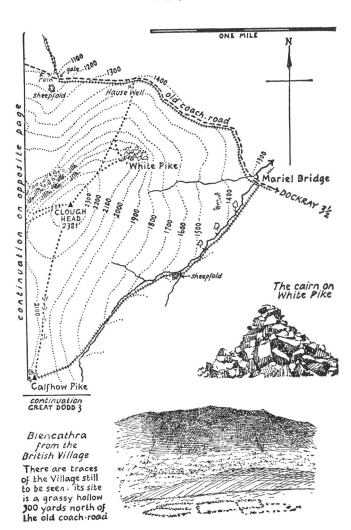

ONE MILE

N

1100
gate 1200
ruin 1300
sheepfold 1400
Hause Well old·coach·road

continuation on opposite page

White Pike

1700
Mariel Bridge
DOCKRAY 3½

CLOUGH HEAD 2381
2300 2200 2100 2000 1900 1800 1700 1600 1500 1400

sheepfold

1100

Calfhow Pike

continuation GREAT DODD 3

The cairn on White Pike

Blencathra from the British Village

There are traces of the Village still to be seen: its site is a grassy hollow 300 yards north of the old coach·road

ASCENT FROM WANTHWAITE
1900 feet of ascent : 2 miles ; 3 by way of Hause Well

'Wanthwaite' is pronounced 'Wanthet'
and 'Lowthwaite' 'Lowthet'

looking east

The adventurous scrambler will enjoy Fisher's Wife's Rake, but the climb is *very* steep. A much easier route is by the grass slope above Hause Well. The intermediate route ends with a choice of paths, one a 'sporting' high-level crossing of the crags to Jim's Fold.

THE SUMMIT

The top of the fell is a pleasant grassy sward, adorned with a small wall-shelter and an Ordnance Survey column.

Skiddaw

DESCENTS: Fisher's Wife's Rake is difficult to locate from above and in any case is too steep to provide a comfortable way down. The high-level path from Jim's Fold is an interesting route to the easier ground below the crags. Easiest of all is the grass slope to the old coach-road at Hause Well.

In bad weather conditions Clough Head is a dangerous place. All steep ground should be avoided and the descent made down the easy grass slope north-north-east to the old coach-road. A descent by Fisher's Wife's Rake should not be contemplated and the natural funnel of Sandbed Gill should be strictly left alone

Two oddities on Clough Head

Unlike most Lakeland springs, which rise from grass, HAUSE WELL issues from a crevice in rocks. It is not easy to locate —its situation is near the fence bounding the old coach-road.

SANDBED GILL, a considerable stream in its rocky gorge, has an empty bed at valley-level.

RIDGE ROUTE

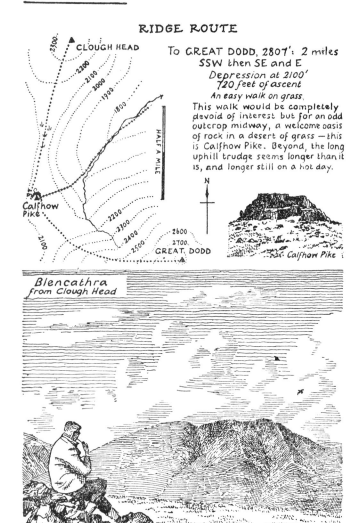

To GREAT DODD, 2807': 2 miles
SSW then SE and E
Depression at 2100'
720 feet of ascent
An easy walk on grass.

This walk would be completely
devoid of interest but for an odd
outcrop midway, a welcome oasis
of rock in a desert of grass — this
is Calfhow Pike. Beyond, the long
uphill trudge seems longer than it
is, and longer still on a hot day.

Calfhow Pike

*Blencathra
from Clough Head*

THE VIEW

Clough Head is sufficiently isolated to afford an uninterrupted prospect in every direction except south-east. A special feature, rare in views from the heights of the Helvellyn range, is the nice combination of valley and mountain scenery. This is an excellent viewpoint, the skyline between south and west being especially striking.

Principal Fells

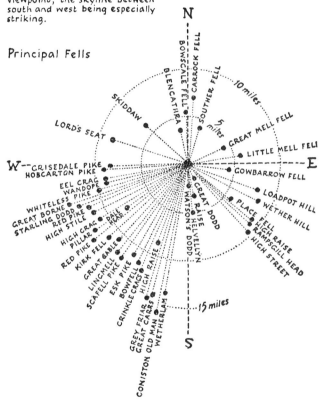

Lakes and Tarns
SW : *Thirlmere*
W : *Derwent Water*
WNW : *Tewet Tarn*
WNW : *Bassenthwaite Lake*

Dollywaggon Pike 2810'

from Deepdale Hause

Patterdale

▲ HELVELLYN

Wythburn

▲ DOLLYWAGGON PIKE
▲ FAIRFIELD

Grasmere

MILES
0   1   2   3   4   5

NATURAL FEATURES

Like most of the high fells south of the Sticks Pass, Dollywaggon Pike exhibits a marked contrast in its western and eastern aspects. To the west, uninteresting grass slopes descend to Dunmail Raise almost unrelieved by rock and scarred only by the wide stony track gouged across the breast of the fell by the boots of generations of pilgrims to Helvellyn. But the eastern side is a desolation of crag and boulder and scree: here are silent recesses rarely visited by walkers but well worth a detailed exploration.

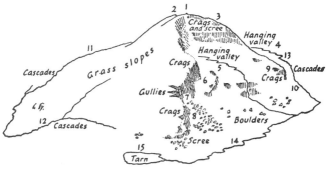

looking north-west

1 The summit of
      Dollywaggon Pike
2 Ridge continuing to
      Nethermost Pike
3 The Tongue
4 Ruthwaite Cove
5 Cock Cove
6 Falcon Crag (or
      Dollywaggon Crag)
7 The three gullies
      of Tarn Crag
8 Tarn Crag
9 Spout Crag
10 Caves (artificial)
11 Birkside Gill
12 Raise Beck
13 Ruthwaite Beck
14 Grisedale Beck
15 Grisedale Tarn

Falcon Crag

The figure 10 also indicates the position of RUTHWAITE LODGE (built in 1854 as a shooting lodge, but now a climbers' hut)

MAP

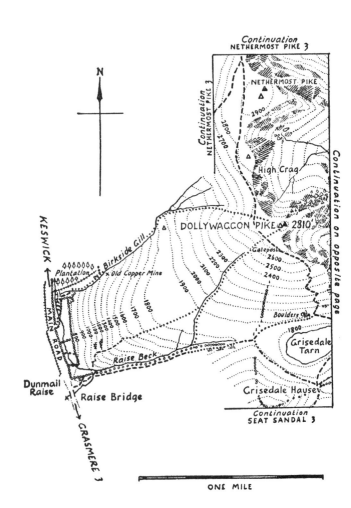

ONE MILE

MAP

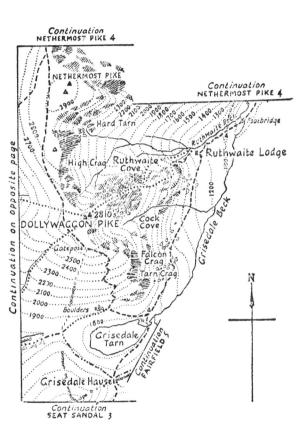

ONE MILE

ASCENT FROM GRASMERE
2700 feet of ascent : 5 miles from Grasmere Church

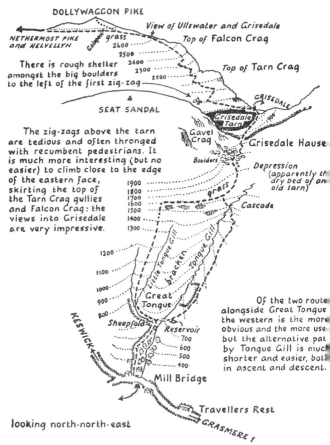

DOLLYWAGGON PIKE

View of Ullswater and Grisedale
Top of Falcon Crag

NETHERMOST PIKE
and HELVELLYN
grass
2600
2500
2400
2300
2200

Top of Tarn Crag

There is rough shelter
amongst the big boulders
to the left of the first zig-zag

GRISEDALE

Grisedale
Tarn

△
SEAT SANDAL

Gavel
Crag

Grisedale Hause

The zig-zags above the tarn
are tedious and often thronged
with recumbent pedestrians. It
is much more interesting (but no
easier) to climb close to the edge
of the eastern face,
skirting the top of
the Tarn Crag gullies
and Falcon Crag: the
views into Grisedale
are very impressive.

Boulders

Depression
(apparently the
dry bed of an
old tarn)

1900
1800
1700
1600
1500
1400
1300

grass

Cascade

1200
1100
1000
900
800

Little Tongue Gill
bracken
Tongue Gill

KESWICK

Great
Tongue

Sheepfold

Reservoir

700
600
500
400

Of the two routes
alongside Great Tongue
the western is the more
obvious and the more used
but the alternative path
by Tongue Gill is much
shorter and easier, both
in ascent and descent.

Mill Bridge

looking north-north-east

Travellers Rest
GRASMERE 1

The route illustrated is the much-trodden path, almost a
highway in places, from Grasmere to Helvellyn. It climbs
the breast of Dollywaggon Pike and passes slightly below
its summit, which is easily attained by a short detour.

ASCENT FROM DUNMAIL RAISE
2100 feet of ascent : 2 miles

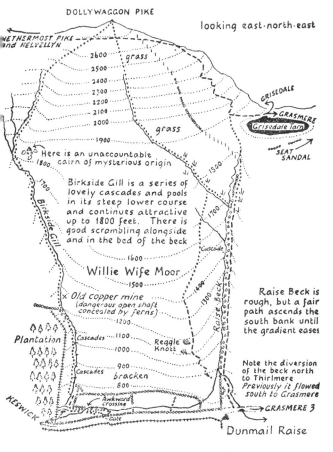

DOLLYWAGGON PIKE

looking east·north·east

NETHERMOST PIKE
and HELVELLYN

2600   grass
2500
2400
2300
2200
2100
2000

1900   grass

*o₅₅ Here is an unaccountable
1800   cairn of mysterious origin*

Birkside Gill is a series of
lovely cascades and pools
in its steep lower course
and continues attractive
up to 1800 feet. There is
good scrambling alongside
and in the bed of the beck

1600

Willie Wife Moor
1500

× *Old copper mine
(dangerous open shaft
concealed by ferns)*
1200

Plantation   Cascades   1100

1000

Cascades   900   bracken

800

Awkward
Crossing

Gate

KESWICK

Birkside Gill   1700

GRISEDALE

GRASMERE
Grisedale Tarn

SEAT
SANDAL

1500

1700

Cascade

Raise Beck   1400

1300

Reggle Knott

Raise Beck is
rough, but a fair
path ascends the
south bank until
the gradient eases

Note the diversion
of the beck north
to Thirlmere
Previously it flowed
south to Grasmere

GRASMERE 3

Dunmail Raise

The western slopes offer a short and direct route from
the main road but are monotonously grassy and of greater
interest to sheep than to walkers. Preferably one of the
two becks should be followed up, especially on a hot day.

ASCENT FROM GRISEDALE
2400 feet of ascent · 5 miles from Patterdale village

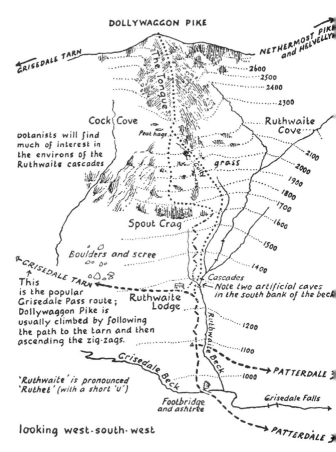

DOLLYWAGGON PIKE

GRISEDALE TARN

NETHERMOST PIKE
and HELVELLYN

2600
2500
2400

2300

The Tongue

Cock Cove

Peat hags

Ruthwaite Cove

botanists will find
much of interest in
the environs of the
Ruthwaite cascades

grass

2100

2000

1900

1800

1700

Spout Crag

1600

1500

Boulders and scree

1400

Cascades

GRISEDALE TARN

This
is the popular
Grisedale Pass route;
Dollywaggon Pike is
usually climbed by following
the path to the tarn and then
ascending the zig-zags.

Ruthwaite
Lodge

Note two artificial caves
in the south bank of the beck

Ruthwaite Beck

1200

1100

PATTERDALE 3

'Ruthwaite' is pronounced
'Ruthet' (with a short 'u')

Grisedale Beck

1000

Grisedale Falls

Footbridge
and ash tree

PATTERDALE 3

looking west-south-west

This is much the most interesting and exhilarating way to
the summit, but it is relatively unknown and rarely used.
The finish up the narrow Tongue is excellent. *This route
should not be attempted in bad weather conditions.*

THE SUMMIT

The summit is a small grassy dome, narrowing to the east. The big cairn is 30 yards west of the highest point.

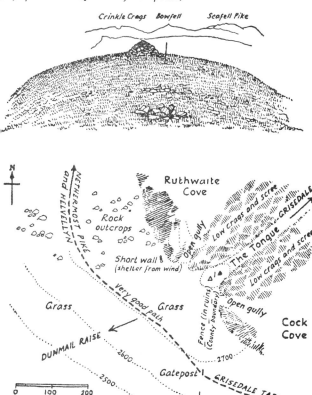

DESCENTS: The quickest and easiest way off is the direct descent to Dunmail Raise, but Birkside Gill should be avoided. The Tongue route should not be attempted, nor descents made into Cock Cove or Ruthwaite Cove, *in mist*: this side of the fell is extremely rough. *In bad weather conditions*, the safest descent is to Grisedale Tarn by the zig-zag path, for either Grasmere or Patterdale.

THE VIEW

The view is extensive in most directions but restricted in the north and south-east by neighbouring fells of greater altitude. Westwards, the panorama is excellent.

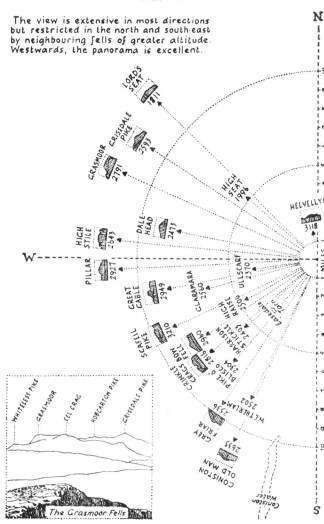

N

LORD'S SEAT 1811

CRISEDALE PIKE 2593

GRASMOOR 2791

HIGH SEAT 1996

HELVELLYN 3118

HIGH STILE 2643

DALE HEAD 2473

PILLAR 2927

CLARAMARA 2560

ULLSCARF 2370

GREAT GABLE 2949

HIGH RAISE 2500

W

SCAFELL PIKE 3210

HARRISON STICKLE 2403

RAISE 2304

EASEDALE TARN

CRINKLE CRAGS 2816

BOW FELL 2960

PIKE O' BLISCO 2304

WETHERLAM 2502

GREY FRIAR 2536

CONISTON OLD MAN 2635

Coniston Water

MILES

S

The Grasmoor Fells

WHITELESS PIKE · GRASMOOR · EEL CRAG · HOBCARTON PIKE · CRISEDALE PIKE

THE VIEW

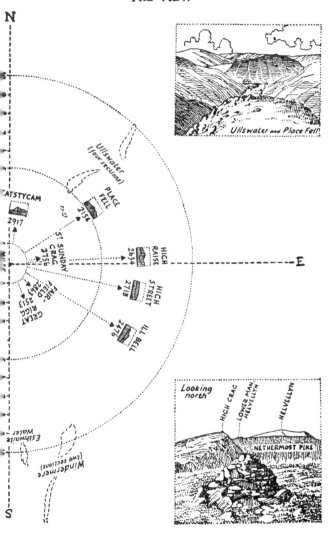

Ullswater and Place Fell

N

E

Ullswater (four sections)

PLACE FELL 2154

CATSTYCAM 2917

ST SUNDAY CRAG 2756

HIGH RAISE 2634

HIGH STREET 2718

FAIR-FIELD 2863

GREAT RIGG 2513

ILL BELL 2476

Esthwaite Water

Windermere (two sections)

S

Looking north

HIGH CRAG
LOWER MAN HELVELLYN
HELVELLYN
NETHERMOST PIKE

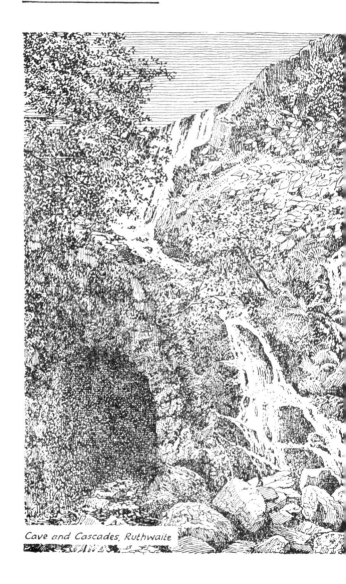

Cave and Cascades, Ruthwaite

RIDGE ROUTES

To NETHERMOST PIKE, 2920' : 1 mile : NW then N.

Depression at 2700'
220 feet of ascent

An easy walk with fine views. Safe in mist if the path is followed closely.

An excellent path links Dollywaggon Pike and Nethermost Pike, skirting their actual summits to the west. A more interesting route (no path) lies along the edge of the crags overlooking Ruthwaite Cove.

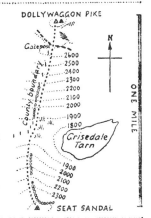

To SEAT SANDAL, 2415'
1¼ miles : S

Depression at 1850'
600 feet of ascent

A steep but easy descent followed by a dull climb. The depression is marshy. Safe but unpleasant in mist.

Seat Sandal is the next fell to the south, but the direct route to it can hardly be called a ridge. There is no path, but the way is indicated by broken fences and walls.

The Tarn Crag gullies

Dove Crag

2603'

from Dovedale

Patterdale •

Hartsop •

▲ FAIRFIELD

DOVE ▲ CRAG

RED SCREES ▲

• Grasmere

Ambleside •

MILES

0 1 2 3 4

The lofty height that towers so magnificently over Dovedale is indebted for its name to a very impressive vertical wall of rock on its north-east flank: the crag was named first and the summit of the parent fell above, which officially is considered unworthy of any title and is nameless on the Ordnance Survey maps, has adopted it by common consent.

NATURAL FEATURES

Dove Crag is a mountain of sharp contrasts. To the east, its finest aspect, it presents a scarred and rugged face, a face full of character and interest. Here, in small compass, is a tangle of rough country, a maze of steep cliffs, gloomy hollows and curious foothills gnarled like the knuckles of a clenched fist, with the charming valley of Dovedale below and the main crag frowning down over all. Very different is its appearance from other directions. A high ridge runs south, with featureless grass slopes flowing down from it to the valleys of Rydale and Scandale. The fell is a vertebra of the Fairfield spine and is connected to the next height in the system, Hart Crag, by a lofty depression.

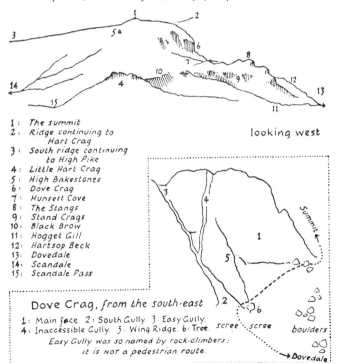

looking west

1: The summit
2: Ridge continuing to Hart Crag
3: South ridge continuing to High Pike
4: Little Hart Crag
5: High Bakestones
6: Dove Crag
7: Hunsett Cove
8: The Stangs
9: Stand Crags
10: Black Brow
11: Hogget Gill
12: Hartsop Beck
13: Dovedale
14: Scandale
15: Scandale Pass

Dove Crag, from the south-east

1: Main face 2: South Gully 3: Easy Gully.
4: Inaccessible Gully 5: Wing Ridge 6: Tree. scree   scree   boulders
Easy Gully was so named by rock-climbers:
it is NOT a pedestrian route.

→ Dovedale

MAP

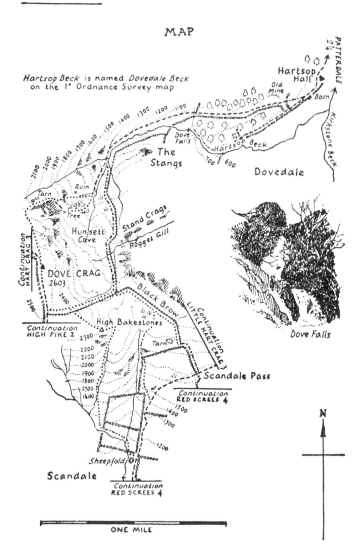

Hartsop Beck is named Dovedale Beck on the 1" Ordnance Survey map

PATTERDALE 24

Hartsop Hall

Old Mine

Barn

Kirkstone Beck

Dove Falls

Hartsop Beck

The Stangs

Dovedale

2100 2000 1900 1800 1700 1600 1500 1400 1300 1200 1100

700 600

Ruin ×

Tarn

Tree

Stand Crags

Hunsett Cove

Hogget Gill

Continuation HART CRAG 3

DOVE CRAG 2603

1800 2100 2200

Black Brow

Continuation LITTLE HART CRAG 3

High Bakestones

Tarn ○

Scandale Pass

Continuation HIGH PIKE 2

2300 2200 2100 2000 1900 1800 1700 1600

Continuation RED SCREES 4

1500 1400 1300

1200

Sheepfold ○

Scandale

Continuation RED SCREES 4

Dove Falls

ONE MILE

N

ASCENT FROM PATTERDALE
2,200 feet of ascent: 5 miles from Patterdale village

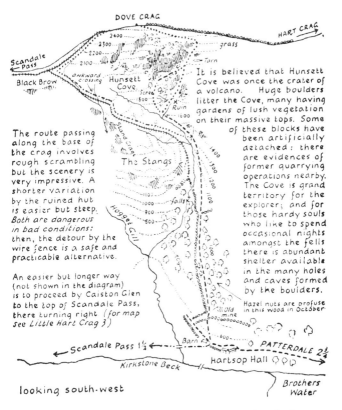

DOVE CRAG

HART CRAG

2400

grass

2300

2200

2100

Scandale Pass

Black Brow

awkward crossing

Hunsett Cove

Tarn

Scree

Ruin

Stand Crag

The Stangs

Hogget Gill

falls

1800

1700

1600

1500

1400

1300

1200

1100

1000

900

800

It is believed that Hunsett Cove was once the crater of a volcano. Huge boulders litter the Cove, many having gardens of lush vegetation on their massive tops. Some of these blocks have been artificially detached: there are evidences of former quarrying operations nearby. The Cove is grand territory for the explorer; and for those hardy souls who like to spend occasional nights amongst the fells there is abundant shelter available in the many holes and caves formed by the boulders.

The route passing along the base of the crag involves rough scrambling but the scenery is very impressive. A shorter variation by the ruined hut is easier but steep. Both are dangerous in bad conditions: then, the detour by the wire fence is a safe and practicable alternative.

An easier but longer way (not shown in the diagram) is to proceed by Caiston Glen to the top of Scandale Pass, there turning right (for map see *Little Hart Crag 3*)

Hazel nuts are profuse in this wood in October

Old mine

Barn

Scandale Pass 1½

PATTERDALE 2¼

Hartsop Hall

Kirkstone Beck

Brothers Water

looking south-west

Dove Crag is most often ascended from Ambleside on the popular tour of the 'Fairfield Horseshoe' —— but the climb from Patterdale, by Dovedale, is far superior: it gives a much more interesting and intimate approach, the sharp transition from the soft loveliness of the valley to the desolation above being very impressive.

ASCENT FROM AMBLESIDE
2500 feet of ascent : 5 miles

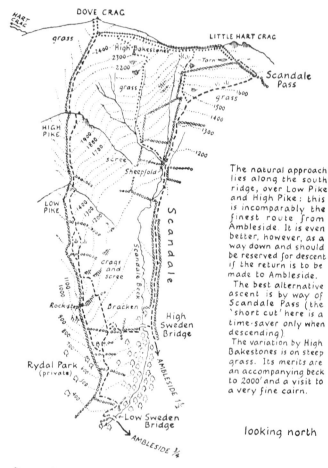

The natural approach lies along the south ridge, over Low Pike and High Pike : this is incomparably the finest route from Ambleside. It is even better, however, as a way down and should be reserved for descent if the return is to be made to Ambleside.

The best alternative ascent is by way of Scandale Pass (the 'short cut' here is a time-saver only when descending)

The variation by High Bakestones is on steep grass. Its merits are an accompanying beck to 2000' and a visit to a very fine cairn.

looking north

Dove Crag cannot be seen from Ambleside, but rising from the fields north of the town is its clearly-defined south ridge, offering an obvious staircase to the summit.

THE SUMMIT

The actual top of the fell is a small rock platform crowned by a cairn, twenty yards east of the crumbling wall crossing the broad summit-plateau. It is of little distinction and there is nothing of interest in the immediate surroundings.

A visit to the top of the crag will repay walkers who have a liking for exploration. A quarter-mile north of the cairn, Easy Gully is reached by following down the natural slope of the fell: it can be identified by an overhang on the wall of the gully. A dividing buttress hides Inaccessible Gully, the upper exit of which will be found forty yards north. Just to the left of the top of Inaccessible Gully is a cross-wall which marks the limit of exploration, for beyond it is the precipitous main face of the crag.

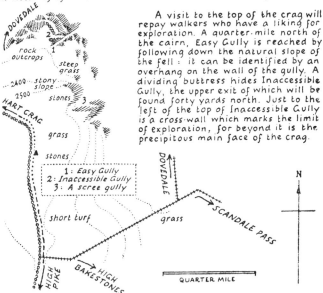

1: Easy Gully
2: Inaccessible Gully
3: A scree gully

DOVEDALE

HART CRAG

rock outcrops
steep grass
2400 stony slope
2500
stones 3
grass
stones

short turf
grass
SCANDALE PASS

HIGH PIKE
HIGH BAKESTONES

QUARTER MILE

N

DESCENTS: All routes of ascent may be reversed for descent but the way down into Dovedale by the base of the crag is very rough. The High Bakestones route to Scandale is not recommended. *In mist*, whether bound for Ambleside or Patterdale, the wall should be followed south, soon turning left along the fence for Patterdale via Dovedale or Scandale Pass. *Direct descents to Dovedale from the summit must not be attempted.*

THE VIEW

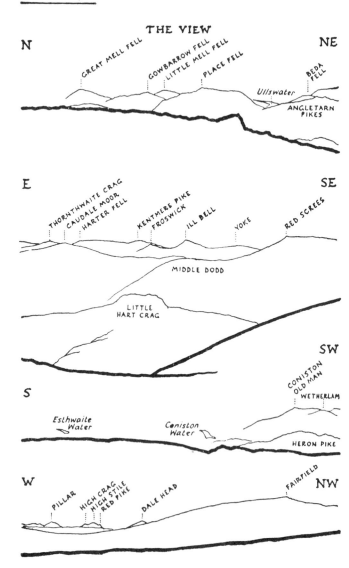

THE VIEW

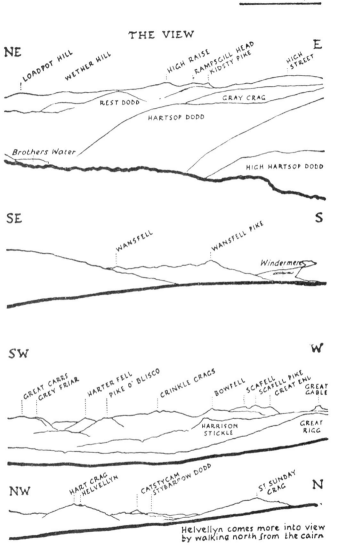

NE

LOADPOT HILL
WETHER HILL
HIGH RAISE
RAMPSGILL HEAD
KIDSTY PIKE
HIGH STREET
E

REST DODD
GRAY CRAG
HARTSOP DODD

Brothers Water
HIGH HARTSOP DODD

SE

S

WANSFELL
WANSFELL PIKE
Windermere

SW

W

GREAT CARRS
GREY FRIAR
HARTER FELL
PIKE O' BLISCO
CRINKLE CRAGS
BOWFELL
SCAFELL
SCAFELL PIKE
GREAT END
GREAT GABLE

HARRISON STICKLE
GREAT RIGG

NW

HART CRAG
HELVELLYN
CATSTYCAM
STYBARROW DODD
St. SUNDAY CRAG
N

Helvellyn comes more into view
by walking north from the cairn

RIDGE ROUTES

To HART CRAG, 2698', ¾ mile : NW
Depression at 2350'
350 feet of ascent

An easy walk. Hart Crag is not safe in mist.

A faint grass path accompanies the wall to the depression; beyond, the wall ends at a cluster of rocks. A track, plain at first, goes steeply up the stony breast of Hart Crag and becomes indistinct on the grass at the top.

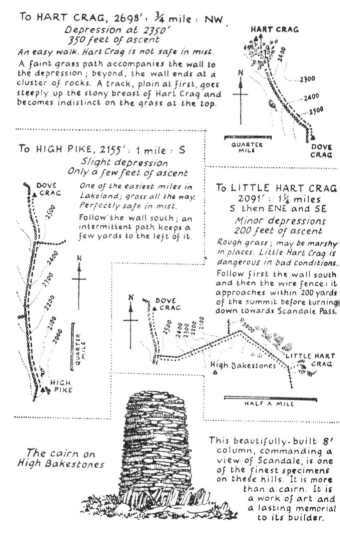

HART CRAG

2400
2300
2400
2500

N

QUARTER MILE

DOVE CRAG

To HIGH PIKE, 2155': 1 mile : S
Slight depression
Only a few feet of ascent

One of the easiest miles in Lakeland; grass all the way. Perfectly safe in mist.

Follow the wall south; an intermittent path keeps a few yards to the left of it.

DOVE CRAG

2500
2400
2300
2200
2100
2000

N

QUARTER MILE

HIGH PIKE

To LITTLE HART CRAG
2091': 1¼ miles
S then ENE and SE
Minor depressions
200 feet of ascent

Rough grass; may be marshy in places. Little Hart Crag is dangerous in bad conditions.

Follow first the wall south and then the wire fence: it approaches within 200 yards of the summit before turning down towards Scandale Pass.

N

DOVE CRAG

2500
2400
2300
2200
2100

2000

High Bakestones

LITTLE HART CRAG

HALF A MILE

The cairn on High Bakestones

This beautifully-built 8' column, commanding a view of Scandale, is one of the finest specimens on these hills. It is more than a cairn. It is a work of art and a lasting memorial to its builder.

Dovedale, from the top of Easy Gully

Fairfield

2863'

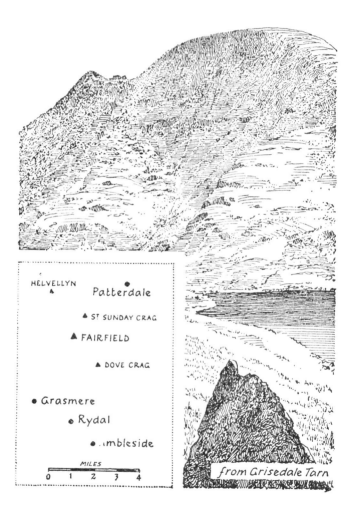

HELVELLYN
▲
Patterdale
●

▲ St SUNDAY CRAG

▲ FAIRFIELD

▲ DOVE CRAG

● Grasmere

● Rydal

● Ambleside

MILES

0 1 2 3 4

from Grisedale Tarn

NATURAL FEATURES

The rough triangle formed by Grisedale Pass, the Rothay valley and Scandale Pass, with the village of Patterdale as its apex, contains within its area a bulky mountain-system with five distinct summits over 2500'. High ridges link these summits; there are also subsidiary ridges and spurs of lesser altitude, massive rocky buttresses, gloomy coves and fine daleheads. The whole mass constitutes a single geographical unit and the main summit is Fairfield, a grand mountain with grand satellites in support. No group of fells in the district exhibits a more striking contrast in appearance when surveyed from opposite sides than this lofty Fairfield group. From the south it appears as a great horseshoe of grassy slopes below a consistently high skyline, simple in design and impressive in altitude, but lacking those dramatic qualities that appeal most to the lover of hills. But on the north side the Fairfield range is magnificent: here are dark precipices, long fans of scree, abrupt crags, desolate combes and deep valleys: a tangle of rough country, small in extent but full of interest, and well worth exploration. This grimmer side of the Fairfield group can only be visited conveniently from the Patterdale area. Fairfield turns its broad back to the south, to Rydal and Grasmere, and climbers from this direction get only the merest glimpse of its best features; many visitors to the summit, indeed, return unsuspecting, and remember Fairfield and its neighbours as mountains of grass. The few who know the head of Deepdale and the recesses of Dovedale, intimately, have a very different impression.

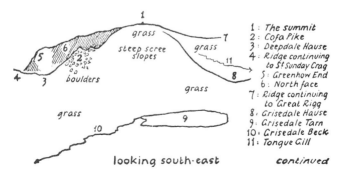

grass

1 — steep scree slopes — 7 — grass — 11

grass

boulders

grass

8

grass

9

grass — 10

1 : The summit
2 : Cofa Pike
3 : Deepdale Hause
4 : Ridge continuing to St Sunday Crag
5 : Greenhow End
6 : North face
7 : Ridge continuing to Great Rigg
8 : Grisedale Hause
9 : Grisedale Tarn
10 : Grisedale Beck
11 : Tongue Gill

looking south-east

continued

NATURAL FEATURES

continued

Three ridges leave the top of Fairfield: one goes south over Great Rigg to end abruptly at Nab Scar above Rydal Water; another, the spine of the Fairfield system, keeps a high level to Dove Crag, traversing Hart Crag on the way, and the third, and best, runs north inclining east over the splintered crest of Cofa Pike and on to St Sunday Crag. On the west flank only is there no descending ridge: here an ill-defined gable-end falls steeply to Grisedale Hause.

The southern and western slopes are simple, the northern and eastern complicated and far more interesting. Here a mile-long face of alternating rock and scree towers high above the barren hollow of Deepdale. Crags abound: most impressive is the precipitous cliff of Greenhow End, scarped on three sides and thrusting far into the valley, and a wall of even steeper rock, with Scrubby Crag prominent, bounds Link Cove to the east.

Fairfield claims Deepdale Beck, Rydal Beck and the main branch of Tongue Gill as its streams, but is only one of many contributors to Grisedale Beck. It is without a tarn of its own, forming one side only of the green basin containing Grisedale Tarn.

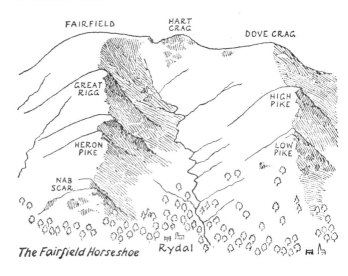

The Fairfield Horseshoe

Cofa Pike and the north-east ridge

Greenhow End

Scrubby Crag

The Crags
of
Fairfield

Black Crag, Rydal Head.

MAP

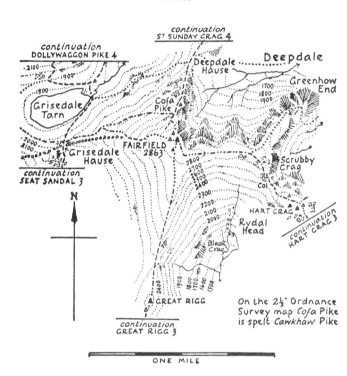

continuation
ST SUNDAY CRAG 4

continuation
DOLLYWAGGON PIKE 4

Deepdale

Deepdale
Hause

Greenhow
End

-2100-
-1900-
-1800-

Grisedale
Tarn

1700
1800
1900

Cofa
Pike

-2000-
-2100-

FAIRFIELD
2863

Grisedale
Hause

Scrubby
Crag

continuation
SEAT SANDAL 3

2800
2700
2600
2500
2400

Col

N

2300

HART CRAG

continuation
HART CRAG 3

2200
2100
2000

Rydal
Head

Black
Crag

1800
1700
1600
1500

1900

2400

GREAT RIGG

continuation
GREAT RIGG 3

On the 2½" Ordnance
Survey map *Cofa Pike*
is spelt *Cawkhaw* Pike

ONE MILE

Rocks on *Cofa Pike*

ASCENT FROM GRASMERE
2650 feet of ascent : 4¼ miles from Grasmere Church

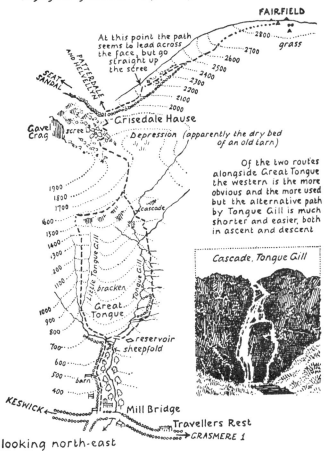

FAIRFIELD

2800

grass

At this point the path
seems to lead across
the face, but go
straight up
the scree

PATTERDALE AND HELVELLYN

2700

2600
2500
2400
2300
2200
2100
2000

SEAT SANDAL

Grisedale Hause

Gavel Crag

scree

Depression (apparently the dry bed
of an old tarn)

Of the two routes
alongside Great Tongue
the western is the more
obvious and the more used
but the alternative path
by Tongue Gill is much
shorter and easier, both
in ascent and descent

1900
1800
1700
1600
1500
1400
1300
1200
1100
1000
900
800
700
600
500
400

cascade

Little Tongue Gill

Tongue Gill

bracken

Great
Tongue

reservoir
sheepfold

barn

KESWICK ←

Mill Bridge

Travellers Rest
→ GRASMERE 1

Cascade, Tongue Gill

looking north-east

The path to Grisedale Hause, by either side of the Tongue,
is distinct but above the Hause it is not so well marked.
Tongue Gill is an interesting approach but the last 1000'
of climbing is dull. The top of Fairfield is confusing in mist.

ASCENT FROM PATTERDALE
2400 feet of ascent : 5½ miles

FAIRFIELD

HART CRAG

Cofa Pike

Deepdale Hause

St SUNDAY CRAG

grass 2700
2600

Link Cove
1900

scree

grass

1000

grass

Greenhow End

1800
1700

grass

sheepfold

Earnest Crag

1600
1500
1400
1300
1200
1100

1500 1600 1700 1800 1900

glacial moraines

Deepdale Beck

bracken

1000

Deepdale

900

bracken

800

sheepfold

450

Wallend

bracken

Deepdale Hall

gate

→ PATTERDALE ¾

KIRKSTONE ←

Bridgend

looking south·west

This is a most impressive approach. The towering cliffs of Greenhow End and the mile·long facade of imposing crags and deep·riven gullies on Fairfield's north·east face are ample recompense for the immediate dreariness of Deepdale.

If the return is to be made to Patterdale over St Sunday Crag (as it should be if the weather is good) the route would have to be retraced as far as Deepdale Hause. This is no disadvantage over such interesting territory, but walkers who object to going over the same ground twice could use the better·known approach along Grisedale to the wall on Grisedale Hause — beyond the tarn — proceeding thence to the top by the Grasmere route; this alternative is easier.

The route over Greenhow End, shown on the diagram, is for experienced scramblers only, *in fine weather.*

The gradual revelation of the savage northern face of Fairfield as the view up Deepdale unfolds gives a high quality to this route. Deepdale itself is desolate, but has interesting evidences of glacial action; Link Cove is one of the finest examples of a hanging valley.

The head of Deepdale

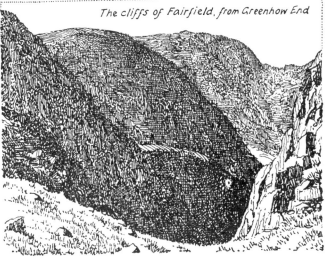

The cliffs of Fairfield, from Greenhow End

THE SUMMIT

The summit of Fairfield is an extensive grassy plateau. The absence of distinguishing natural features makes it, in mist, particularly confusing, and the abundance of cairns is then a hindrance rather than a help. The actual top is flat and its surface is too rough to bear the imprint of paths, and the one definable point is a tumbledown windbreak of stones, built as a short wall and offering shelter only to persons of imagination. Thirty yards in front of the shelter is the principal and largest cairn, standing almost on the rim of the steep north face. Mention should be made of the excellent turf on this wide top: weary feet will judge it delightful.

DESCENTS : Too many cairns are worse than too few, and it is unfortunate that the tops of the buttresses of the north face are unnecessarily adorned with piles of stones, snares in mist for strangers to the fell, who may think they indicate ways off the summit. So they do — sudden ways off. There is no trouble in clear weather in identifying the various routes of descent, the best of which lies over Cofa Pike and St Sunday Crag to Patterdale : an exhilarating and beautiful walk.

In mist, note that none of the usual routes descend over steep ground and that a cairn does not necessarily indicate a path. With care, all routes are quite practicable, but the safest way off, in bad weather and whatever the destination, is westwards to Grisedale Tarn, following a line of cairns until a path appears. (It doesn't matter much about finding a path if the walker is sure he is going either west or south, or between these points, but he who wanders northward courts disaster)

THE SUMMIT

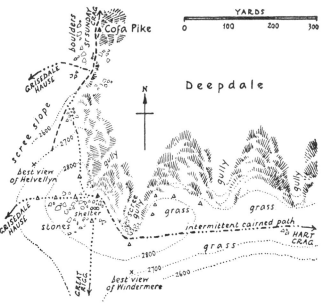

Travellers along the path to Hart Crag are urged to leave it, *in clear weather,* and skirt the edge of the cliffs just to the north, the peeps of Deepdale down the gullies being very impressive. A detour to the top of Greenhow End, easily reached by a gradual descent over grass, is highly recommended, the rock-scenery being especially good and the arete attractive. *This place is dangerous in mist.*

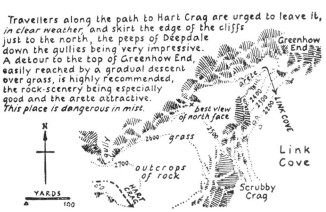

THE VIEW

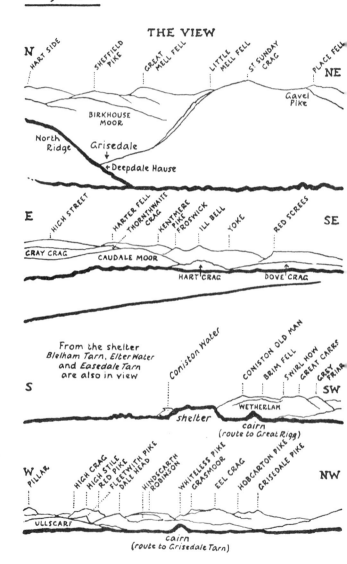

From the shelter
Blelham Tarn, Elter Water
and Easedale Tarn
are also in view

cairn
(route to Great Rigg)

cairn
(route to Grisedale Tarn)

THE VIEW

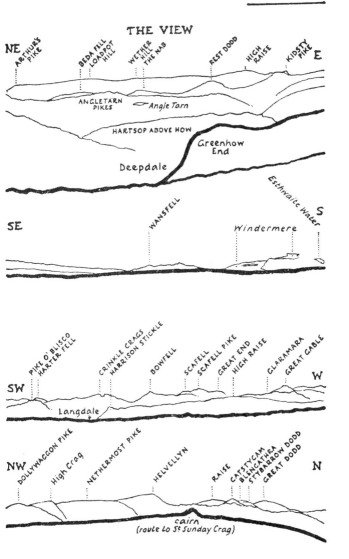

RIDGE ROUTES

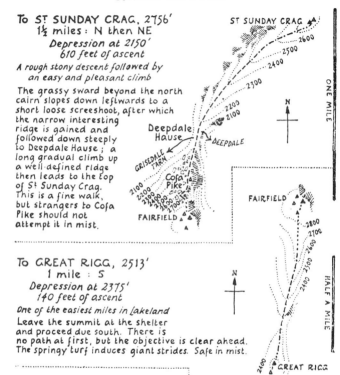

To ST SUNDAY CRAG, 2756'
1½ miles : N then NE
Depression at 2150'
610 feet of ascent

A rough stony descent followed by an easy and pleasant climb

The grassy sward beyond the north cairn slopes down leftwards to a short loose screeshoot, after which the narrow interesting ridge is gained and followed down steeply to Deepdale Hause; a long gradual climb up a well-defined ridge then leads to the top of St Sunday Crag. This is a fine walk, but strangers to Cofa Pike should not attempt it in mist.

ST SUNDAY CRAG

ONE MILE

Deepdale Hause
DEEPDALE
GRISEDALE TARN
Cofa Pike
FAIRFIELD

FAIRFIELD

To GREAT RIGG, 2513'
1 mile : S
Depression at 2375'
140 feet of ascent

One of the easiest miles in Lakeland

Leave the summit at the shelter and proceed due south. There is no path at first, but the objective is clear ahead. The springy turf induces giant strides. Safe in mist.

HALF A MILE

GREAT RIGG

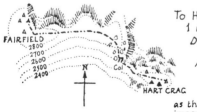

FAIRFIELD
Col
HART CRAG

HALF A MILE

To HART CRAG, 2698'
1 mile : E then SE
Depression at 2550'
150 feet of ascent

An easy, interesting walk.

The path across the broad top of Fairfield is cairned but indistinct; it improves as the col is approached. It is important, in mist, not to stray from the path : danger lurks!

The north face of Fairfield

Glenridding Dodd

1425'
approx.

from Ullswater
(Sheffield Pike behind)

Glencoyne •

GLENRIDDING DODD
▲

Glenridding •

Patterdale •

MILES
0   1   2

Fashions change. When people climbed hills only for the sake of the views, the heathery summit of Glenridding Dodd must have been more frequented than it is today, for once-popular paths of ascent are now overgrown and neglected. It occupies a grand position overlooking the upper reach of Ullswater. It is the end, topographically, of the eastern shoulder of Stybarrow Dodd.

MAP

HALF A MILE

ASCENT FROM GLENRIDDING
1000 feet of ascent

The Dodd is so conveniently situated and offers so delightful a view that it might be expected that walkers would have blazed a wide path to the top. Such is not the case, however, and it is not at all easy to find a route that does not involve a minor trespass. The upper slopes are largely defended by woodlands and a wall which frustrated tourists have broken in places. The most straightforward route climbs steeply by the left (west) of Blaes Crag (*see diagram, Sheffield Pike 4*); the most pleasant traverses the fell above the wall and ascends by Mossdale Beck. The path *through* the woods to the wall, shown on the map, is overgrown and difficult to follow when the bracken is high.

THE SUMMIT

On a sunny day in August the summit is a delectable place. It is richly clothed with heather, and larches almost reach the top on the north side. Many cairns adorn the hummocky summit, the main one overlooking Glenridding village.

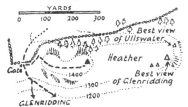

Stybarrow Crag.

THE VIEW

Considering the low altitude of the fell, the view is very pleasing: it gains in charm and intimacy what it lacks in extensiveness. Ullswater takes pride of place.

Principal Fells

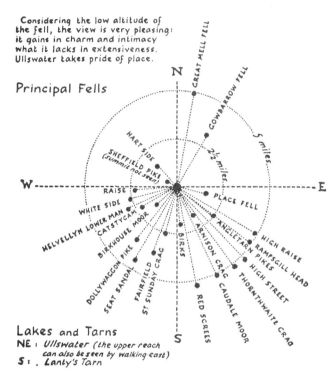

Lakes and Tarns

NE : *Ullswater* (the upper reach can also be seen by walking east)
S : *Lanty's Tarn*

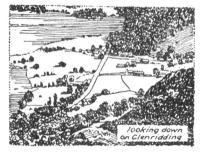

looking down on Glenridding

Ullswater and Birk Fell

from Brown Hills

▲ GREAT MELL FELL
Pooley
Bridge ●
LITTLE
MELL ▲
FELL
● Watermillock
▲ GOWBARROW FELL
● Dockray

● Glenridding
MILES
0 1 2 3 4

NATURAL FEATURES

Gowbarrow Fell is one of the best known of Lakeland's lesser heights, much of it being National Trust property and a favourite playground and picnic place. It is not the fell itself that brings the crowds, however, and its summit is lonely enough: the great attraction is Aira Force, on the beck forming its western boundary. The fell springs from a mass of high dreary ground in the north and takes the shape of a broad wedge, tapering as it falls to Ullswater, the middle reach of which is its south-eastern boundary throughout. The delightful lower slopes here are beautifully wooded, but low crags and bracken in abundance make them rather difficult of access except where they are traversed by the many pleasant green paths which add so much to Gowbarrow's charms.

The Head of Ullswater
from Green Hill

MAP

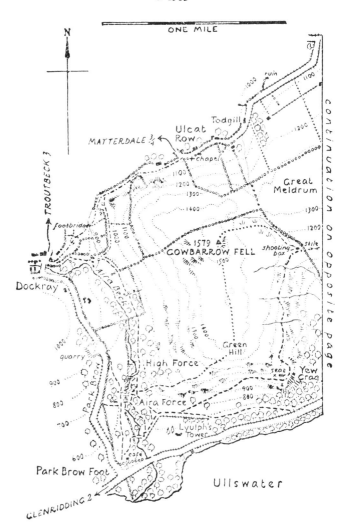

MAP

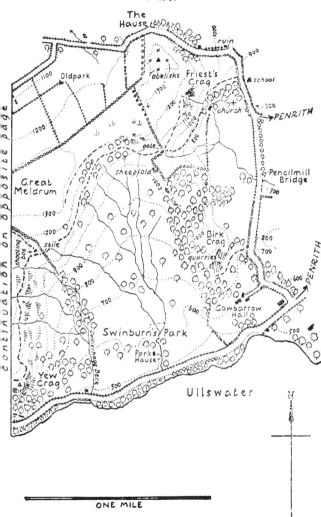

ONE MILE

Aira Force

Waterfalls.
Aira Beck

High Force

Place Fell
and Ullswater
from Gowbarrow Park

ASCENTS

From Park Brow Foot (the usual starting-place for the climb) a path can be seen rising across the fellside behind Lyulph's Tower to the cairn above Yew Crag: this is the best way to the summit. The path, always interesting, continues to the shooting-box (there is shelter here) and then goes upstream to be lost in marshes with the summit-cairn plainly in sight a quarter-mile distant. (The shooting-box may be reached also by a pleasant but overgrown path that starts behind Watermillock Church) A shorter route from Park Brow Foot goes up the shoulder above Aira Force, but the path comes to an early end. The ascent from Dockray direct (by following up the wall) is much less attractive.

Cairn above Yew Crag

Yew Crag

The Shooting-box

THE SUMMIT

Great Mell Fell

Flowers, heather and bilberries bloom on the pleasant little ridge where stands the summit-cairn, but the neighbourhood is drab. This ridge is fringed on the side facing Ullswater by a wall of short broken crags and there are other outcrops nearby.

DESCENTS: The best way off the fell is over the undulating top to Green Hill, descending from there to Aira Force. If the bracken is high, it is worth while to search for the path.

In mist, join the wall north of the cairn, turning left for Dockray, right for the shooting box (for either Watermillock or Park Brow Foot).

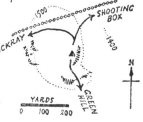

1500
SHOOTING BOX
DOCKRAY
1400
GREEN HILL
N
YARDS
0   100   200

NOTE: Although the altitude of the summit is commonly accepted as 1579', the 2½" Ordnance Survey map (but not the 1") shows a 1600' contour, probably in error.

The summit-ridge

THE VIEW

Gowbarrow Fell faces up Ullswater into the throat of the deep valley of Patterdale, and a feature of the view is the impressive grouping of the fells steeply enclosing it. Very little of the lake can be seen from the top of the fell because of the intervening high ground. Half a mile south from the cairn is a far better viewpoint, Green Hill.

Principal Fells

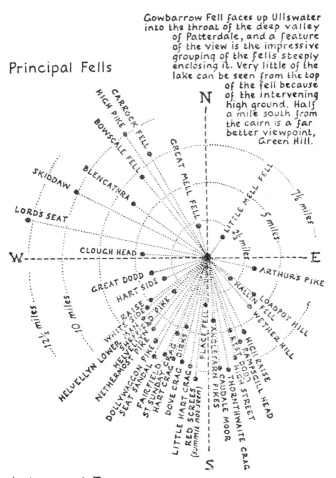

Lakes and Tarns

ENE : Ullswater — the lower reach only. The more attractive upper reaches come into view by walking across the top to Green Hill, where the lake is seen most impressively.

Great Dodd

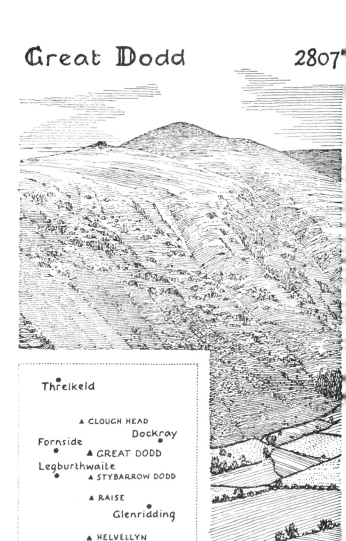

Threlkeld

▲ CLOUGH HEAD

Dockray

Fornside
●

▲ GREAT DODD

Legburthwaite
●

▲ STYBARROW DODD

▲ RAISE

● Glenridding

▲ HELVELLYN

MILES

0   1   2   3   4

from High Rigg

NATURAL FEATURES

Great Dodd, well named, is the most extensive of the fells in the Helvellyn range. To the north-east, its long sprawling slopes fall away gradually in an undulating wilderness of grass to the old coach-road; beyond is a wide expanse of uncultivated marshland, not at all characteristic of Lakeland and of no appeal to walkers. North and south, high ground continues the line of the main ridge, but steepening slopes reach valley-level on both east and west flanks. Grass is everywhere: it offers easy and pleasant tramping but no excitements. Rocks are few and far between: there is a broken line of cliffs, Wolf Crags, overlooking the coach road, and the rough breast of High Brow above Dowthwaitehead breaks out in a series of steep crags (a favourite haunt of buzzards), while there are sundry small outcrops on both east and west flanks well below the summit.

Two of Great Dodd's streams are harnessed to provide water supplies: on the west side, Mill Gill, which has a fine ravine, is diverted to Manchester via Thirlmere; on the east, Aira Beck's famous waterfalls are robbed of their full glory to supply rural districts in Cumberland. Mosedale Beck and Trout Beck drain the dreary wastes to the north.

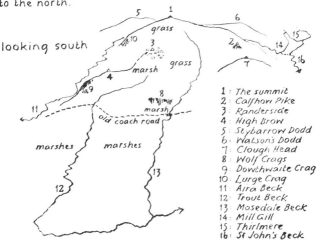

looking south

1 : The summit
2 : Calfhow Pike
3 : Randerside
4 : High Brow
5 : Stybarrow Dodd
6 : Watson's Dodd
7 : Clough Head
8 : Wolf Crags
9 : Dowthwaite Crag
10 : Lurge Crag
11 : Aira Beck
12 : Trout Beck
13 : Mosedale Beck
14 : Mill Gill
15 : Thirlmere
16 : St John's Beck

MAP

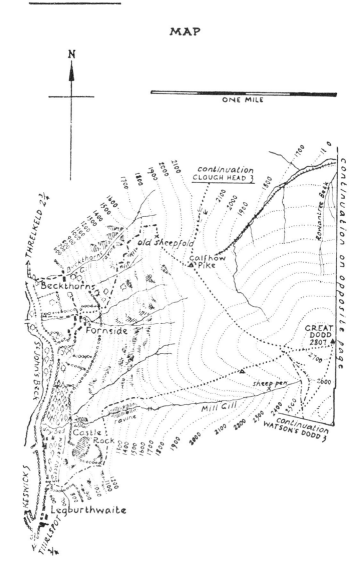

N

ONE MILE

MAP

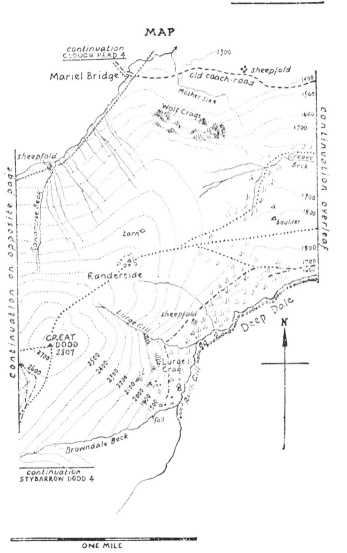

ONE MILE

MAP

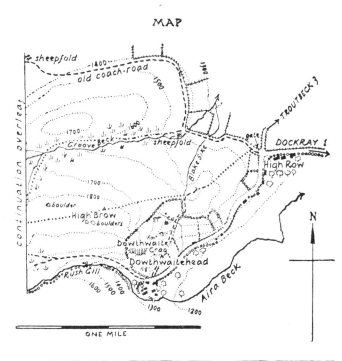

ONE MILE

Wolf Crags

ASCENT FROM DOCKRAY
2000 feet of ascent · 4¾ miles

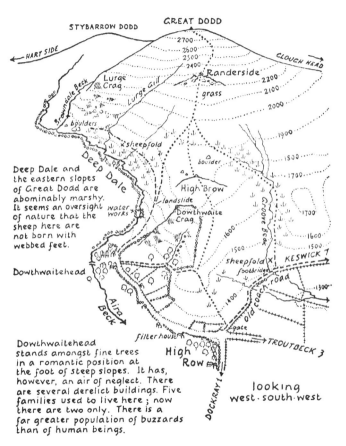

Deep Dale and
the eastern slopes
of Great Dodd are
abominably marshy.
It seems an oversight
of nature that the
sheep here are
not born with
webbed feet.

Dowthwaitehead
stands amongst fine trees
in a romantic position at
the foot of steep slopes. It has,
however, an air of neglect. There
are several derelict buildings. Five
families used to live here; now
there are two only. There is a
far greater population of buzzards
than of human beings.

looking
west·south·west

The ascent of Great Dodd via Groove Beck is one of
the easiest climbs in Lakeland, the gradients being
very gentle throughout, but otherwise it is without
merit. All routes from Dockray are uninspiring and
dreary, and most unpleasant in wet weather.

ASCENT FROM FORNSIDE
2300 feet of ascent : 2½ miles

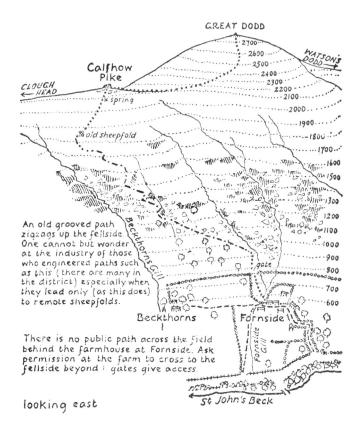

An old grooved path
zigzags up the fellside.
One cannot but wonder
at the industry of those
who engineered paths such
as this (there are many in
the district) especially when
they lead only (as this does)
to remote sheepfolds.

There is no public path across the field
behind the farmhouse at Fornside. Ask
permission at the farm to cross to the
fellside beyond: gates give access.

looking east

This route is very rarely used. It is steep as far as
the sheepfold, but there is recompense in the lovely
view of the valley above Fornside. Thereafter it is
monotonously grassy, with only the oddity of Calfhow
Pike to relieve the tedium of progress.

ASCENT FROM LEGBURTHWAITE
2300 feet of ascent : 2¼ miles

*Users of Bartholomew's map
should note that Legburthwaite is not indicated thereon*

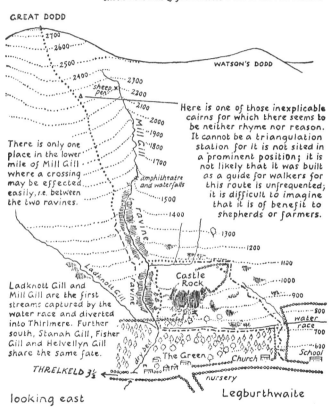

GREAT DODD

2700
2600
2500
2400
2300
2200
2100
2000
1900
1800
1700

WATSON'S DODD

sheep. x
pen

Mill Gill

There is only one
place in the lower
mile of Mill Gill
where a crossing
may be effected
easily, i.e. between
the two ravines.

amphitheatre
and waterfalls

1500

1400

Here is one of those inexplicable
cairns for which there seems to
be neither rhyme nor reason.
It cannot be a triangulation
station for it is not sited in
a prominent position; it is
not likely that it was built
as a guide for walkers for
this route is unfrequented;
it is difficult to imagine
that it is of benefit to
shepherds or farmers.

ravine

1300
1200
1100

Ladknott Gill

Castle
Rock

1000
900

Ladknott Gill and
Mill Gill are the first
streams captured by the
water race and diverted
into Thirlmere. Further
south, Stanah Gill, Fisher
Gill and Helvellyn Gill
share the same fate.

THRELKELD 3½

dry bed

The Green

Church

nursery

800
water
race
700
600
School

Legburthwaite

looking east

The first part of this route is pleasant enough; it
is interesting also if combined with an exploration
of the environs of Castle Rock, but after crossing
the attractive Mill Gill it develops into a trudge
up a long grass slope : the gradient is easy.

THE SUMMIT

The builders of the cairn must have felt twinges of conscience during their task : they selected as its site a most convenient rash of stones, ignoring the highest point a hundred yards distant, where all is grass except for a naked stone thrusting through the turf, its superior altitude unrecognised. The cairn is hollowed to provide shelter from the west wind. The summit is otherwise featureless.

DESCENTS : Grassy slopes fall away gently on all sides. Distances are greater than they seem hereabouts, but progress is rapid. There are no paths from the summit, but in clear weather all routes are easily determined.

In mist, direction may be taken from the shelter in the cairn, which faces east. There is no danger in leaving the top even in the thickest weather, but care must be taken to avoid descending into the inhospitable valley of Deep Dale by mistake.

The cairn on Randerside

Clough Head

The cairn on High Brow

Hart Side   Stybarrow Dodd   Great Dodd

Deep Dale

RIDGE ROUTES

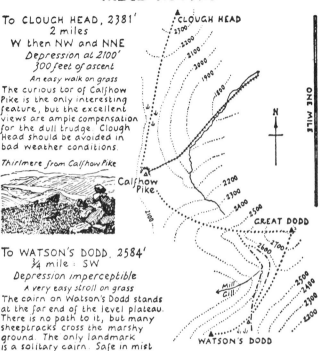

To CLOUGH HEAD, 2381'
2 miles
W then NW and NNE
Depression at 2100'
300 feet of ascent

An easy walk on grass

The curious tor of Calfhow Pike is the only interesting feature, but the excellent views are ample compensation for the dull trudge. Clough Head should be avoided in bad weather conditions.

Thirlmere from Calfhow Pike

To WATSON'S DODD, 2584'
¾ mile : SW
Depression imperceptible

A very easy stroll on grass

The cairn on Watson's Dodd stands at the far end of the level plateau. There is no path to it, but many sheeptracks cross the marshy ground. The only landmark is a solitary cairn. Safe in mist

Dowthwaitehead

THE VIEW

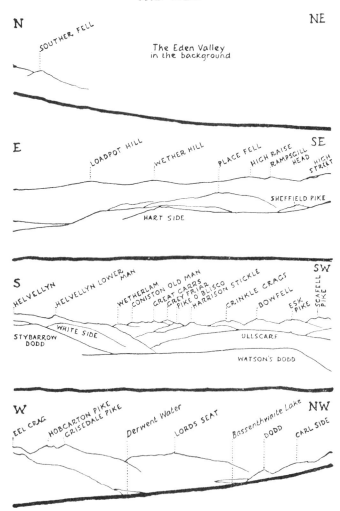

THE VIEW

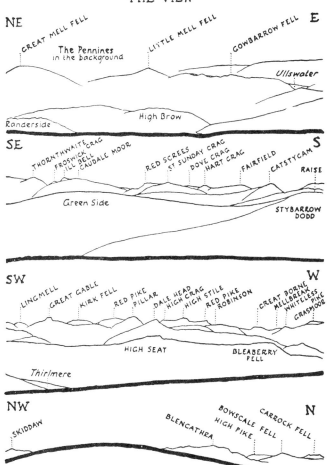

NOTES : This is the view from the cairn,
not from the higher ground to the north.
Thirlmere, Derwent Water and Bassenthwaite Lake
cannot actually be seen from the cairn, but come
into view a few yards to the west.

Great Mell Fell

from Great Meldrum

Troutbeck • Penruddock

GREAT ▲ MELL FELL

      ▲ LITTLE
      MELL
      FELL

Matterdale End •

    ▲ GOWBARROW
    FELL

Dockray •

MILES

0   1   2   3   4

Great Mell Fell is a prominent object on the Penrith approach to Lakeland. With its lesser twin, Little Mell Fell, it forms the portals to the Helvellyn range on this side. Its round 'inverted pudding-basin' shape does not promise much for the walker and it is rarely climbed. On closer acquaintance, however, it is rather more enjoyable than its appearance suggests, because of the presence of fine woodlands on the lower slopes; indeed, pines and larches persist almost to the summit. (But closer acquaintance is frowned upon by the military authorities, who stake a claim here)

NATURAL FEATURES

Great Mell Fell rises sharply from a wide expanse of desolate marshland to the north and west, territory not at all typical of Lakeland, the fell itself being much more fertile and colourful than its surroundings. Its rich red soil carries a wealth of timber, the eastern slopes especially being beautifully wooded. Bleached skeletons of trees near the top of the fell indicate that at one time it was more fully clothed; many of those that yet survive are battered by the prevailing wind into grotesque shapes.

MAP

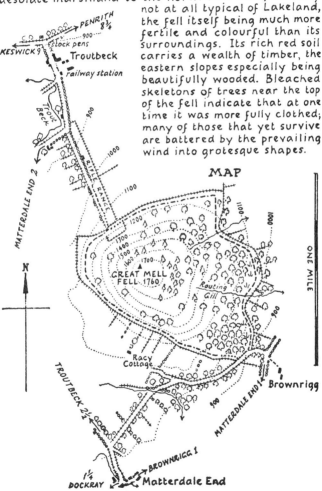

PENRITH 8¾
KESWICK 9
stock pens
Troutbeck
railway station
Trout Beck
MATTERDALE END 2
RIVER RANGE
900
900
1000
1100
1200
1300
1400
1500
1600
1700
GREAT MELL FELL 1760
Routing Gill
1000
1011
1000
900
ONE MILE
N
Racy Cottage
Brownrigg
TROUTBECK 2½
MATTERDALE END 1
900
¼
DOCKRAY
BROWNRIGG 1
Matterdale End

ASCENTS

Above the 1100' contour, roughly, the fell is enclosed within a fence. Access may be gained at Troutbeck (along a muddy lane) and at two gates at the southeastern corner. Each entrance is guarded by red danger signs. Prudent pedestrians will heed the warning and take no further interest in this page. What follows is therefore exclusively for the walker who (a) holds his life cheaply, or (b) reacts to such signs as a bull to a red rag.

A fair path makes a circuit of the fell inside the fence and it may be left anywhere for the climb to the top, the south slope being easiest if a route is selected clear of trees and bracken. The path itself gives a pleasant walk all the way round, but is excessively wet on the eastern side and, in places, overgrown by bracken. Beware flying ammunition, of course.

THE SUMMIT

Tough grass, interspersed with heather, covers the level top. A decayed tree-trunk, appropriately, indicates the highest point, and there are a few unexpected and unhappy stones, looking quite out of their element.

DESCENTS: A way down to the path may be made in any direction but note that the lower east slope is marshy and overgrown. Firing squads, if on duty, are more likely to be met on the north side.

the highest tree

THE VIEW

The highlight of the view is Blencathra undoubtedly, the noble proportions of this fine mountain being seen to great advantage. Otherwise the panorama is uneven, with a wide expanse of the Eden Valley, an impressive grouping of fells southwards, and a vista of the Grasmoor range in the west.

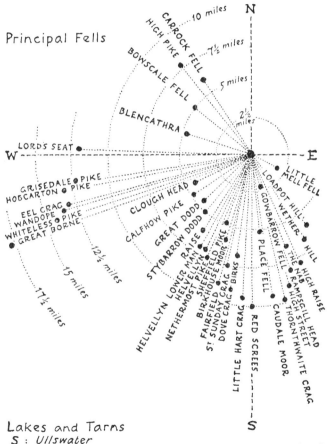

Principal Fells

Lakes and Tarns

S : *Ullswater*
    (a disappointing view, only a very small section being visible)

Great Rigg 2513'

▲ FAIRFIELD

▲ GREAT RIGG

▲ STONE ARTHUR

▲ HERON PIKE

Grasmere • ▲ NAB SCAR

• Rydal

Ambleside •

MILES
0 1 2 3 4

from Grasmere

NATURAL FEATURES

Great Rigg has no topographical secrets or surprises. It is a plain, straightforward, uninteresting fell on the southern spur of Fairfield, with gentle declivities linking the summit to the continuing ridge on either side. East, stony slopes fall abruptly to Rydal Beck; ruined crags rise from wastes of scree. To the west the fellside is mainly grassy but there are occasional rocks low down on this flank, above Tongue Gill. From the ridge south of the summit a descending shoulder strikes off in the direction of Grasmere; this has a rocky terminus with the name of Stone Arthur. Between the shoulder and the ridge is a deep, narrow trough which carries Greenhead Gill, Great Rigg's only stream of note, down to the River Rothay.

Few people will climb Great Rigg without also ascending Fairfield, for the former is a stepping stone to its bigger neighbour. Whilst providing this humble service, however, the fell manages to retain a certain dignity, appreciated best from the west shore of Grasmere: seen from there, the dark dome of its summit appears to overtop all else.

The east face

looking north

gra::

1 The summit
2 Ridge continuing
    to Fairfield
3 Ridge continuing
    to Heron Pike
4 Stone Arthur
5 East face
6 Greenhead Gill
7 Tongue Gill
8 River Rothay

MAP

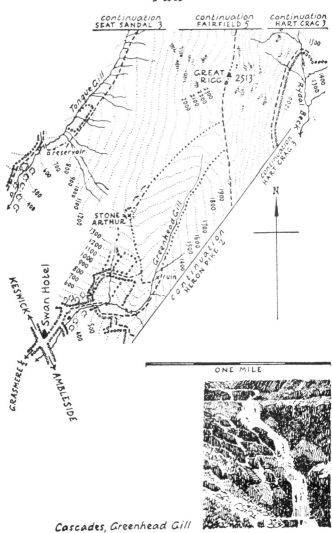

continuation SEAT SANDAL 3
continuation FAIRFIELD 5
continuation HART CRAG 3

GREAT RIGG 2513'

Tongue Gill

reservoir

STONE ARTHUR

Greenhead Gill

continuation HART CRAG 3

Rydal Beck

continuation HERON PIKE 2

x ruin

KESWICK

Swan Hotel

GRASMERE ½

AMBLESIDE

N

ONE MILE

Cascades, Greenhead Gill

ASCENT FROM GRASMERE
2300 feet of ascent : 3 miles

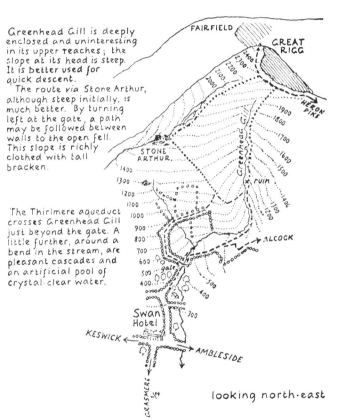

Greenhead Gill is deeply enclosed and uninteresting in its upper reaches; the slope at its head is steep. It is better used for quick descent.

The route *via* Stone Arthur, although steep initially, is much better. By turning left at the gate, a path may be followed between walls to the open fell. This slope is richly clothed with tall bracken.

The Thirlmere aqueduct crosses Greenhead Gill just beyond the gate. A little further, around a bend in the stream, are pleasant cascades and an artificial pool of crystal-clear water.

FAIRFIELD

GREAT RIGG

HERON PIKE

STONE ARTHUR

ruin

ALCOCK

gate

Swan Hotel

KESWICK ←

→ AMBLESIDE

GRASMERE

looking north-east

Great Rigg is more often visited on the tour of the Fairfield Horseshoe, but it may be ascended directly from Grasmere by the routes illustrated, that by Stone Arthur being the more interesting.

THE SUMMIT

Helvellyn   Fairfield

The summit is comprehended at a glance. A well-constructed symmetrical cairn occupies the highest point and another is 60 yards south, where the ridge steepens on its descent to Heron Pike. The top is a carpet of excellent turf which many a cricket-ground would welcome

RIDGE ROUTES

To FAIRFIELD, 2863' : 1 mile : N
Depression at 2375' : 500 feet of ascent
    An easy climb, needing care in mist
A fair path, on grass, crosses the depression but peters out as the summit is approached. Strangers to Fairfield should avoid it in mist.

To HERON PIKE, 2003' : 1½ miles SSW, then S
Minor depressions : 150 feet of ascent
A very easy high-level walk. Heron Pike is the *second* prominent rise on the ridge.

To STONE ARTHUR, 1652' 1¼ miles : SSW then SW
    Downhill all the way
Follow the wide grass shoulder branching from the main ridge. No path. Not quite safe in mist.

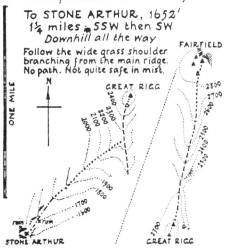

ONE MILE

N

FAIRFIELD

GREAT RIGG

2800
2700
2400
2300
2200
2100
2000
1900
1800
1700
1600

STONE ARTHUR   ruin   x ruin

GREAT RIGG

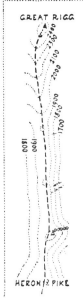

GREAT RIGG

2300
2200
2100
2000
1900
1800
1700
1900
1800
1700

HERON PIKE

THE VIEW

The panorama is interesting and varied,
a special feature being the large number
of lakes and tarns in view. To the
west, the mountain skyline is fine
and there is an impressive vista of
the Helvellyn group above the deep
notch of Grisedale Hause

Principal Fells

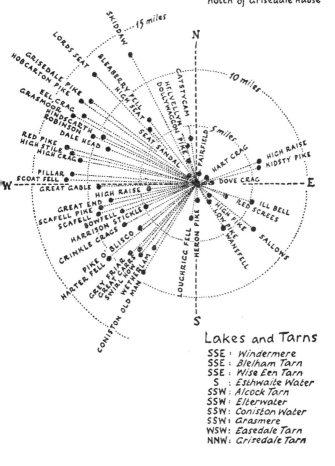

Lakes and Tarns

SSE : *Windermere*
SSE : *Bleiham Tarn*
SSE : *Wise Een Tarn*
 S : *Esthwaite Water*
SSW : *Alcock Tarn*
SSW : *Elterwater*
SSW : *Coniston Water*
SSW : *Grasmere*
WSW : *Easedale Tarn*
NNW : *Grisedale Tarn*

Hart Crag

Patterdale ●

Hartsop ●

FAIRFIELD ▲
HART ▲ CRAG
DOVE CRAG▲

RED SCREES ▲

● Grasmere

● Rydal
Ambleside
●

MILES
0   1   2   3   4

from Dovedale

NATURAL FEATURES

Midway along the high-level traverse between Fairfield and Dove Crag is the rough top of Hart Crag, occupying a strategic position overlooking three valleys. To the north-east, Hart Crag follows usual mountain structure by sending out a long declining ridge, which forms a high barrier between desolate Deepdale and delectable Dovedale. North, a wall of crags defends the summit above the wild hollow of Link Cove, a hanging valley encompassed by cliffs: this is its finest aspect by far. South-west, after an initial fringe of broken crags, long stony slopes fall very steeply to Rydal Head. Although bounded by streams, Hart Crag itself is quite curiously deficient in water-courses.

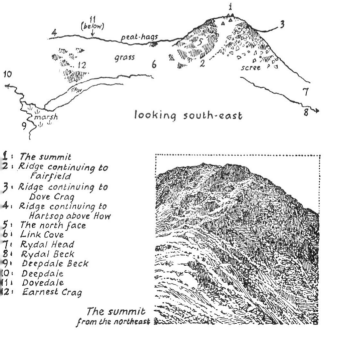

looking south-east

1: The summit
2: Ridge continuing to
   Fairfield
3: Ridge continuing to
   Dove Crag
4: Ridge continuing to
   Hartsop above How
5: The north face
6: Link Cove
7: Rydal Head
8: Rydal Beck
9: Deepdale Beck
10: Deepdale
11: Dovedale
12: Earnest Crag

The summit
from the northeast

MAP

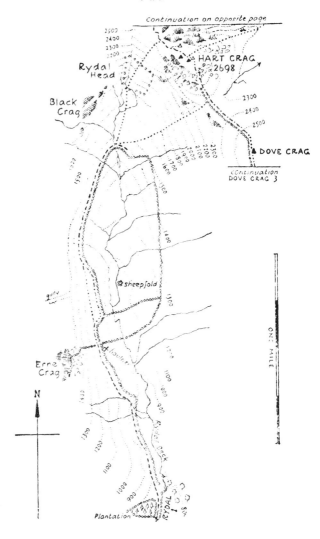

Continuation on opposite page

HART CRAG
2698

Rydal
Head

Black
Crag

DOVE CRAG

Continuation
DOVE CRAG 3

sheepfold

gully

Erne
Crag

N

ONE MILE

Plantation

MAP

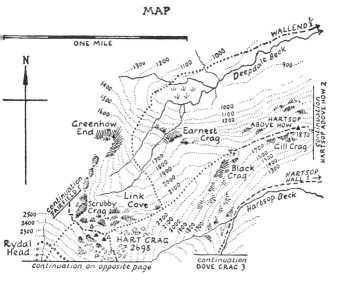

ONE MILE

N

1300 1200 1100 1000

Deepdale Beck

900

WALLEND

continuation HARTSOP ABOVE HOW 2

1400
1500
1600

Greenhow
End

Earnest
Crag

1000
1100
1200

HARTSOP
ABOVE HOW

1870

Gill Crag

1700 1600 1500 1400 1300

HARTSOP
HALL 1

1700
1800
1900

Black
Crag

2000
2100

Link
Cove

continuation FAIRFIELD

Scrubby
Crag

2100

2100
2000
1800 1700

Hartsop Beck

2500
2400
2300

Rydal
Head

HART CRAG
2698

continuation
DOVE CRAG 3

continuation on opposite page

The north face

ASCENT FROM RYDAL
2.600 feet of ascent : 4½ miles

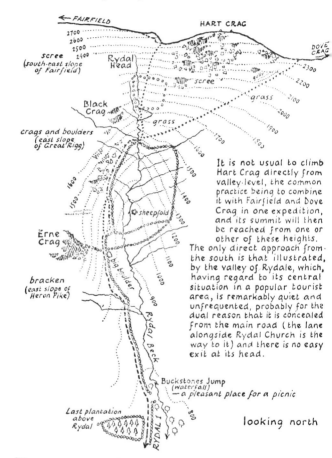

It is not usual to climb Hart Crag directly from valley-level, the common practice being to combine it with Fairfield and Dove Crag in one expedition, and its summit will then be reached from one or other of these heights.

The only direct approach from the south is that illustrated, by the valley of Rydale, which, having regard to its central situation in a popular tourist area, is remarkably quiet and unfrequented, probably for the dual reason that it is concealed from the main road (the lane alongside Rydal Church is the way to it) and there is no easy exit at its head.

looking north

The approach by the Rydal Valley (Rydale) is attractive and interesting, but the climb out of it is very steep. The valley lies entirely within the circuit of the 'Fairfield Horseshoe' and is deeply enclosed.

ASCENT FROM PATTERDALE
2,300 feet of ascent : 4½ miles from Patterdale village

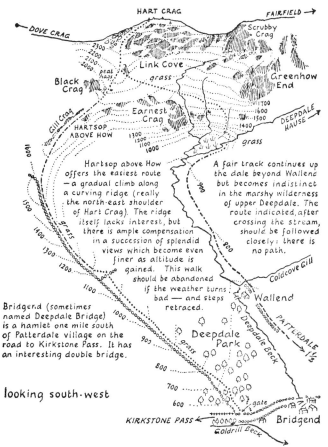

HART CRAG

FAIRFIELD →

Scrubby Crag

DOVE CRAG

2300
2200
2100
2000
peat hags

Link Cove
grass

Black Crag

Greenhow End

Gill Crag

Earnest Crag

1700
1600
1500
1400

DEEPDALE HAUSE

HARTSOP ABOVE HOW

1300
1200
1100
1000

grass

Hartsop above How offers the easiest route — a gradual climb along a curving ridge (really the north-east shoulder of Hart Crag). The ridge itself lacks interest, but there is ample compensation in a succession of splendid views which become even finer as altitude is gained. This walk should be abandoned if the weather turns bad — and steps retraced.

A fair track continues up the dale beyond Wallend but becomes indistinct in the marshy wilderness of upper Deepdale. The route indicated, after crossing the stream, should be followed closely: there is no path.

1600

1500

1400

1300

1200

1100

grass

Coldcove Gill

900

800

Wallend

PATTERDALE

Bridgend (sometimes named Deepdale Bridge) is a hamlet one mile south of Patterdale village on the road to Kirkstone Pass. It has an interesting double bridge.

1000

Deepdale Park

Deepdale Beck

PATTERDALE 1⅓

looking south-west

900

grass

800

700

600

gate

KIRKSTONE PASS ←

Goldrill Beck

Bridgend

The ascent from Patterdale is far superior to that from the south. The Link Cove route especially is an interesting climb through the inner sanctuary of Hart Crag, the scene being impressive, but it is quite unsuitable in bad weather.

THE SUMMIT

The summit area is relatively small, its level top being about 120 yards long and having a cairn at each end. Two other cairns indicate viewpoints. The top is stony but a strip of grass running lengthwise across it to the north of the main cairns offers an easy traverse

Link Cove

FAIRFIELD

crags

HARTSOP ABOVE HOW (in clear weather only)

Col

grass

RYDALE (no path)

2600

2400

boulders

N

2500

2698

HARTSOP ABOVE HOW (in clear weather only)

DESCENTS:
For Patterdale direct, the best way down in good weather is by the long ridge of Hartsop above How: an easy grass descent. The Link Cove route has no merit as a way off. For Rydal direct, the easier route is to descend from the depression between Hart Crag and Dove Crag, the slope here being less steep than that below the Fairfield-Hart Crag col.

Hart Crag can be a dangerous place in mist, the path across the summit being indistinct. Attempts to descend to Link Cove should not be considered. In emergency, aim for the depression between Hart Crag and Dove Crag. A safe descent from here may be made to Rydale, and, with care, to Dovedale. The wall is a safe guide to Ambleside.

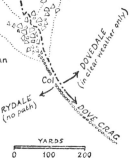

Col

DOVEDALE (in clear weather only)

RYDALE (no path)

DOVE CRAG

YARDS
0   100   200

THE VIEW

Hart Crag is a little too near to the great mass of Fairfield to provide a well-balanced view. The panorama in other directions is extensive, but the picture as a whole is disappointing.

Principal Fells

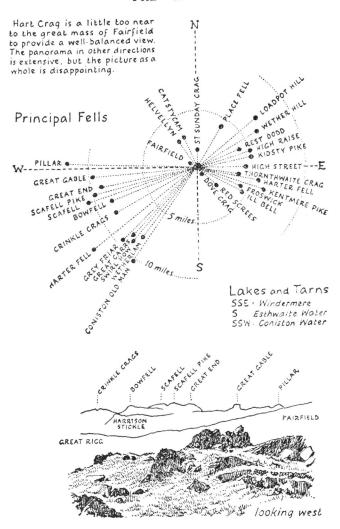

N

CATSTYCAM
HELVELLYN
ST SUNDAY CRAG
PLACE FELL
LOADPOT HILL
WETHER HILL
REST DODD
HIGH RAISE
KIDSTY PIKE
FAIRFIELD

W PILLAR — HIGH STREET — E
GREAT GABLE
THORNTHWAITE CRAG
HARTER FELL
GREAT END
KENTMERE PIKE
SCAFELL PIKE
FROSWICK
SCAFELL
RED SCREES
ILL BELL
BOWFELL
DOVE CRAG

CRINKLE CRAGS
5 miles

HARTER FELL
GREY FRIAR
GREAT CARRS
SWIRL HOW
WETHERLAM
10 miles
S

CONISTON OLD MAN

Lakes and Tarns

SSE · Windermere
S · Esthwaite Water
SSW · Coniston Water

CRINKLE CRAGS
BOWFELL
SCAFELL
SCAFELL PIKE
GREAT END
GREAT GABLE
PILLAR

HARRISON
STICKLE
FAIRFIELD

GREAT RIGG

looking west

RIDGE ROUTES

To FAIRFIELD, 2863' : 1 mile : NW, then W.
Depression at 2550' : 330 feet of ascent

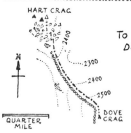

FAIRFIELD

2800
2700
2600
2500
2400

Scrubby Crag

Col

HART CRAG

N

HALF A MILE

An easy walk, but in bad weather Fairfield is dangerous to anyone unfamiliar with the ground and should then be avoided.

A good path crosses the grassy depression and climbs the stony slope opposite to the big plateau of Fairfield's summit. The track here is indistinct and indicated by many cairns; excellent turf.

HART CRAG

2400

2300

2400

2500

N

DOVE CRAG

QUARTER MILE

To DOVE CRAG, 2603' : ¾ mile : SE.
Depression at 2350' : 260 feet of ascent

An easy walk. Dove Crag is safe in mist, but care is then necessary in leaving Hart Crag.

An indistinct path, at first over grass and then, more clearly, among stones goes south from the eastern cairn to the wall at the depression. This wall continues over the summit of Dove Crag

To HARTSOP ABOVE HOW, 1870' : 1½ miles : ENE
Depression at 1775' : 150 feet of ascent

An easy walk. In mist the correct way off Hart Crag is not easy to find (there is no path) and this walk should not then be attempted.

Leave the summit near the main cairn, going down a patch of grass and crossing a band of scree before inclining slightly right down a shallow stony gully. Then work left to the ridge, which is broad and grassy, with many undulations and peat-hags. It narrows on the final rise.

HARTSOP
ABOVE HOW

Gill Crag

Black Crag

N

2000 1900 1800 1700

2300

2200

2100

HART CRAG

Note that this ridge may be safely left only between Black Crag and Gill Crag (by descending right, to Dovedale)

ONE MILE

from the east ridge, St Sunday Crag

Hart Side   2481'

from Dockray

GREAT
DODD ▲   ● Dockray

▲ HART SIDE

STYBARROW   ● Glencoyne
DODD ▲

● Glenridding

MILES
0   1   2   3

NATURAL FEATURES

The main watershed at Stybarrow Dodd sends out a long spur to the east which curves north from the subsidiary height of Green Side and continues at an elevated level until it is poised high above Ullswater before descending in wide slopes to the open country around Dockray. The principal height on this spur is Hart Side, which with its many satellites on the declining ridge forms the southern wall of the long valley of Deep Dale throughout its sinuous course, its opposite boundary being the short deep trench of Glencoyne. The upper slopes of this bulky mass are unattractive in themselves, but, in strong contrast, the steep flank overlooking Ullswater is beautifully wooded, while the views of the lake from the Brown Hills, midway along the ridge, are of high quality.

Hart Side is rarely visited. Its smooth slopes, grass and marsh intermingling, seem very very remote from industry, but there are evidences that men laboured on these lonely heights a long time ago, and even now the minerals far below its surface are being won by the enterprising miners of Glenridding.

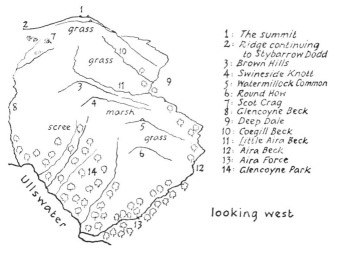

1: The summit
2: Ridge continuing to Stybarrow Dodd
3: Brown Hills
4: Swineside Knott
5: Watermillock Common
6: Round How
7: Scot Crag
8: Glencoyne Beck
9: Deep Dale
10: Coegill Beck
11: Little Aira Beck
12: Aira Beck
13: Aira Force
14: Glencoyne Park

looking west

MAP

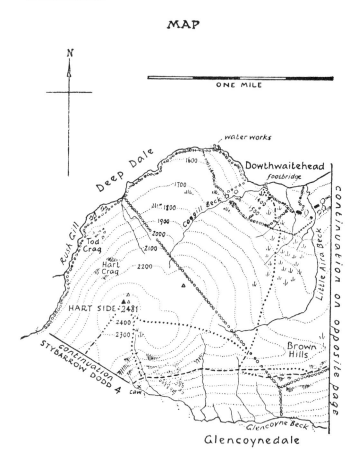

According to the Ordnance Survey and Bartholomew's maps, the representation of a footpath thereon is no evidence of a right of way. Nor, unfortunately, is it evidence that a footpath now exists at all! Some of the paths marked on those maps in the district of Hart Side were made originally by miners on their way to or from work at the Glenridding lead mine, but the miners now use them no more: they have become overgrown and cannot, in many places, be traced.

MAP

TROUTBECK 3

Dockray

Aira Beck

Round How

Quarry

Park Brow

gate

Common Fell

900

800

Watermillock Common

700

Little Aira Beck

Glencoyne Park

café

Swineside Knott

1800

Brown Hills

x fold

1500
1400
1300
1200
1100
1000
900

Ullswater

800
700
600

Glencoyne Beck

Glencoyne

GLENRIDDING 1

N

ONE MILE

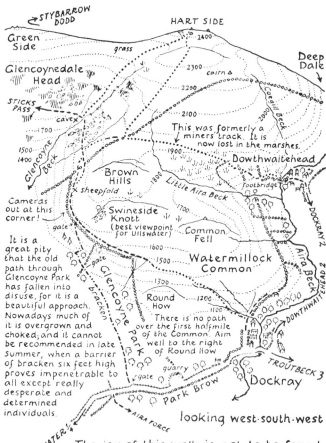

ASCENT FROM DOCKRAY
1600 feet of ascent : 4 miles

→STYBARROW DODD

HART SIDE

Green Side

grass

2400

Deep Dale

Glencoynedale Head

2300

cairn △

2200

Coalgill Beck

STICKS PASS

cavex

2100

This was formerly a miners' track. It is now lost in the marshes.

1700

1900

Dowthwaitehead

1500
1400

Glencoyne Beck

Brown Hills

1800

Little Aira Beck

footbridge

sheepfold

DOCKRAY 2

Cameras out at this corner!

gate

Swineside Knott (best viewpoint for Ullswater)

1700

Common Fell

It is a great pity that the old path through Glencoyne Park has fallen into disuse, for it is a beautiful approach. Nowadays much of it is overgrown and choked; and it cannot be recommended in late summer, when a barrier of bracken six feet high proves impenetrable to all except really desperate and determined individuals.

gate

Glencoyne Park

bracken

1600

1500

Watermillock Common

1300

Round How

1200

1100

There is no path over the first halfmile of the Common. Aim well to the right of Round How

Aira Beck

DOWTHWAITEHEAD 2

quarry

gate

Park Brow

TROUTBECK 3

Dockray

→AIRA FORCE

looking west·south·west

←ULLSWATER!

The joy of this walk is not to be found in the summit of Hart Side, which is dull, but in the splendid high·level route to it along the Brown Hills, which excels in views of Ullswater. The alternative shown deserves no consideration.

THE SUMMIT

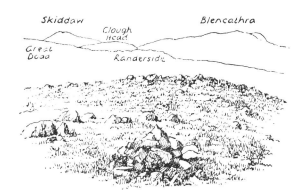

Skiddaw   Clough Head   Blencathra
Great Dodd   Randerside

The summit has nothing extraordinary to show in natural forms, being grassy with a few outcropping boulders. Yet this is a top that cannot be confused with any other, for here man has not contented himself merely with building a few cairns but has really got to work with pick and spade, and excavated a most remarkable ditch, rather like the Vallum of the Roman Wall. As the project was abandoned, the reason for the prodigious effort is not clear. An excavation below the summit, intended as the site of a building, was similarly abandoned.

excavation
×   △
△   2632
△   DOCKRAY
ditch

100 YARDS

Probably these were workings for the Glenridding lead mine, as is a cave in Glencoynedale Head, near the miners' path: here a warning notice — "Danger. Keep Out" — relieves the duly grateful guide-book writer of the task of exploring its fearsome interior.

The ditch on the summit

DESCENTS: Descents will usually be either to Dockray or Glencoyne. Walk ESE, over a minor rise, to the wall running across the fell. Follow the wall down, joining the miners' path (at a gap) for Dockray. For Glencoyne, continue by the wall down into the valley. These are the best routes in mist.

The cave

RIDGE ROUTE

To STYBARROW DODD, 2770'
1½ miles: SW then W
Depressions at 2250' and 2525'
550 feet of ascent

An easy walk on grass. Safe in mist.
Follow round the head of Deep Dale,
skirting the intermediate summit
of Green Side. In mist, take care
to keep the rising slope on the left.

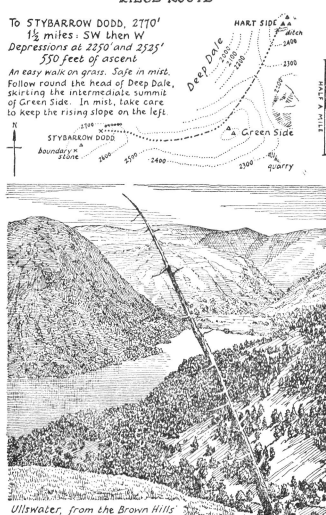

Ullswater, from the Brown Hills

THE VIEW

Principal Fells

The view is disappointing. Although Hart Side has a considerable altitude, it does not overtop the main ridge to the west, which hides all the high fells beyond. Intervening ground to the east conceals most of Ullswater.

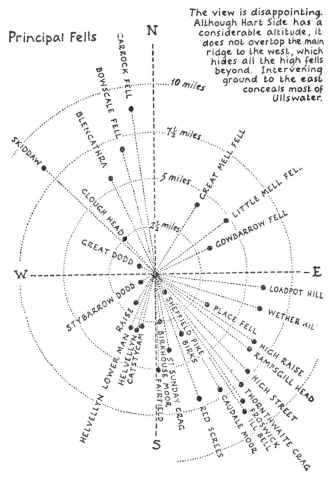

Lakes and Tarns
ENE : Ullswater

from Hunsett Cove

Patterdale •

St SUNDAY
CRAG ▲   Hartsop
                      •
FAIRFIELD   ▲HARTSOP
▲   ABOVE HOW
HART CRAG ▲

            ▲ DOVE CRAG

MILES
0   1   2   3

The long curving northeast ridge of Hart Crag rises to a separate summit midway, and this summit is generally referred to as Hartsop above How by guidebook writers and mapmakers. Sometimes the three words in the name are hyphenated, sometimes not. Probably the first two should be, but not the last two: the word 'How' is common, meaning a low hill, and the distinctive title of this particular How is 'Hartsop-above', indicating its geographical relationship to the hamlet in the valley below. Most natives of Deepdale, however, know it not by this name, with or without hyphens, but they all know Gill Crag, which fringes the summit, and this would seem to be a more satisfactory name for the fell. But one cannot so wantonly ignore the authority of the guidebooks and maps; and the name Hartsop above How, without hyphens (in the belief that an error of omission is a less sin than an error of commission) will be used here in support of the Director General of Ordnance Survey.

NATURAL FEATURES

Hartsop above How is a simple ridge (really a part of Hart Crag) curving like a sickle to enclose the valley of Deepdale on the south and east. Only in the vicinity of the summit is it at all narrow, but both flanks are steep throughout most of its three-mile length, the slopes above Dovedale being especially rough. There are several crags on the fell, the most imposing being Black Crag above the rough hollow of Hunsett Cove ; also prominent are the grey rocks of Dovedale Slabs (looking as pleasant and attractive as steep rocks can look) below the eastern end of the summit, and, on the Deepdale side, the gloomy cliff of Earnest Crag (looking as unpleasant and unattractive as steep rocks can look). The slopes above Brothers Water are well-wooded over an extensive area, and Deepdale Park also has some fine trees.

MAP

ASCENT FROM PATTERDALE
1400 feet of ascent : 3 miles from Patterdale village

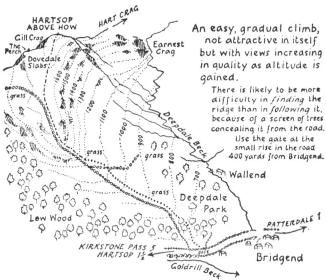

An easy, gradual climb, not attractive in itself but with views increasing in quality as altitude is gained.

There is likely to be more difficulty in *finding* the ridge than in *following* it, because of a screen of trees concealing it from the road. Use the gate at the small rise in the road 400 yards from Bridgend.

looking south-west

Dovedale Slabs

THE SUMMIT

The highest point is a grassy knoll adjoining the top of a cleft splitting Gill Crag, but the usually accepted summit is 200 yards northeast and bears a small cairn.

DESCENTS : The easiest way down *in any conditions* is by the ridge to the road. Direct descents, either to Deepdale or Dovedale, are too rough.

THE VIEW

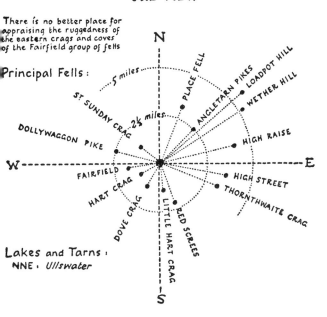

There is no better place for appraising the ruggedness of the eastern crags and coves of the Fairfield group of fells

Principal Fells:

ST SUNDAY CRAG
DOLLYWAGGON PIKE
FAIRFIELD
HART CRAG
DOVE CRAG
LITTLE HART CRAG
RED SCREES
PLACE FELL
ANGLETARN PIKES
LOADPOT HILL
WETHER HILL
HIGH RAISE
HIGH STREET
THORNTHWAITE CRAG

5 miles
2½ miles

N
W — E
S

Lakes and Tarns:
NNE: Ullswater

RIDGE ROUTE

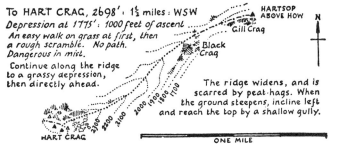

To HART CRAG, 2698': 1½ miles: WSW
Depression at 1775': 1000 feet of ascent
An easy walk on grass at first, then a rough scramble. No path. Dangerous in mist.
Continue along the ridge to a grassy depression, then directly ahead.

HARTSOP ABOVE HOW
Gill Crag
Black Crag

N

The ridge widens, and is scarred by peat-hags. When the ground steepens, incline left and reach the top by a shallow gully.

2300 2200 2100 2000 1900 1800 1700

HART CRAG

ONE MILE

Helvellyn

3118'

from the south-west ridge of St Sunday Crag

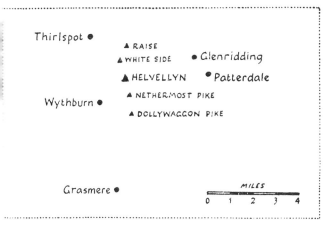

Legend and poetry, a lovely name and a lofty altitude combine to encompass Helvellyn in an aura of romance; and thousands of pilgrims, aided by its easy accessibility, are attracted to its summit every year. There is no doubt that Helvellyn is climbed more often than any other mountain in Lakeland, and, more than any other, it is the objective and ambition of the tourist who does not normally climb; moreover, the easy paths leading up the western flanks make it particularly suitable for sunrise expeditions, and, in a snowy winter, its sweeping slopes afford great sport to the ski parties who congregate on these white expanses. There are few days in any year when no visitor calls at the wall-shelter on the summit to eat his sandwiches. It is a great pity that Helvellyn is usually ascended by its western routes, for this side is unattractive and lacking in interest. From the east, however, the approach is quite exciting, with the reward of an extensive panorama as a sudden and dramatic climax when the top is gained; only to the traveller from this direction does Helvellyn display its true character and reveal its secrets. There is some quality about Helvellyn which endears it in the memory of most people who have stood on its breezy top; although it can be a grim place indeed on a wild night, it is, as a rule, a very friendly giant. If it did not inspire affection would its devotees return to it so often?

NATURAL FEATURES

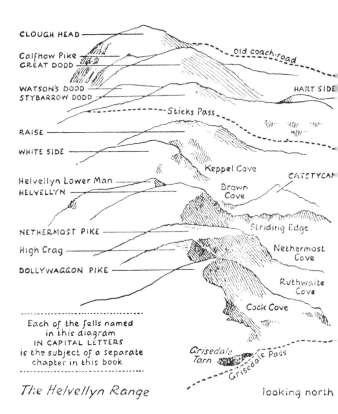

CLOUGH HEAD

Calfhow Pike
GREAT DODD

Old coach-road

WATSON'S DODD
STYBARROW DODD

HART SIDE

Sticks Pass

RAISE

WHITE SIDE

Keppel Cove

CATSTYCAM

Helvellyn Lower Man
HELVELLYN

Brown
Cove

NETHERMOST PIKE

Striding Edge

High Crag

Nethermost
Cove

DOLLYWAGGON PIKE

Ruthwaite
Cove

Cock Cove

Each of the fells named
in this diagram
IN CAPITAL LETTERS
is the subject of a separate
chapter in this book

Grisedale
Tarn

Grisedale Pass

The Helvellyn Range

looking north

The altitude of these fells and the main connecting ridge
is consistently above 2500 feet from Dollywaggon Pike (2810',
to Great Dodd (2807') except for the depression of Sticks Pass
which is slightly below. This is the greatest area of high fells
in Lakeland, and the traverse of the complete range from south
to north (the better way) is a challenge to all active walkers.
(As a preliminary canter, strong men will include the Fairfield group,
starting at Kirkstone Pass and reaching Grisedale Tarn over the tops
of Red Screes, Little Hart Crag, Dove Crag, Hart Crag and Fairfield)

NATURAL FEATURES

The Helvellyn range is extremely massive, forming a tremendous natural barrier from north to south between the deep troughs of the Thirlmere and Ullswater valleys. The many fells in this vast upland area are each given a separate chapter in this book, and the following notes relate only to Helvellyn itself, with its main summit at 3118' (the third highest in Lakeland) and a subsidiary at 3033'.

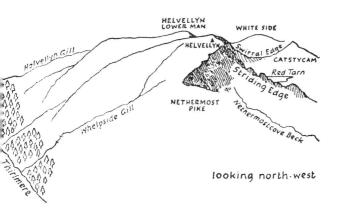

looking north-west

Helvellyn is a high point on a high ridge and therefore is substantially buttressed by neighbouring heights, the connecting depressions, north and south, being relatively slight. Westwards, however, after a gentle incline from the summit the slope quickens and finally plunges steeply down to Thirlmere, the total fall in height being nearly half a mile in a lateral distance of little more than one mile. This great mountain wall below the upper slopes is of simple design, consisting of two broad buttresses each bounded by swift-flowing streams and scarred by broken crags and occasional scree gullies. The base of the slope is densely planted with conifers.

continued

NATURAL FEATURES

continued

The smooth slopes curving up from the west break abruptly along the ridge, where, in complete contrast, a shattered cliff of crag and scree falls away precipitously eastwards : here are the most dramatic scenes Helvellyn has to offer. From the edge of the declivity on the summit Red Tarn is seen directly below, enclosed between the bony arms of Swirral Edge on the left and Striding Edge on the right. Swirral Edge terminates in the grassy cone of Catstycam, a graceful peak, but Striding Edge is all bare rock, a succession of jagged fangs ending in a black tower. The Edges are bounded by deep rough hollows, silent and very lonely. Beyond the Edges is the bulky mass of Birkhouse Moor, Helvellyn's long east shoulder, a high wedge separating Grisedale and Glenridding and descending to the lovely shores of Ullswater.

Striding Edge

Early writers regarded Striding Edge as a place of terror; contemporary writers, following a modern fashion, are inclined to dismiss it as of little account. In fact Striding Edge is the finest ridge there is in Lakeland, for walkers — its traverse is always an exhilarating adventure in fair weather or foul, and it can be made easy or difficult according to choice. The danger of accident is present only when a high wind is blowing or when the rocks are iced : in mist on a calm day, the Edge is a really fascinating place.

Swirral Edge

Helvellyn from Red Tarn

MAP

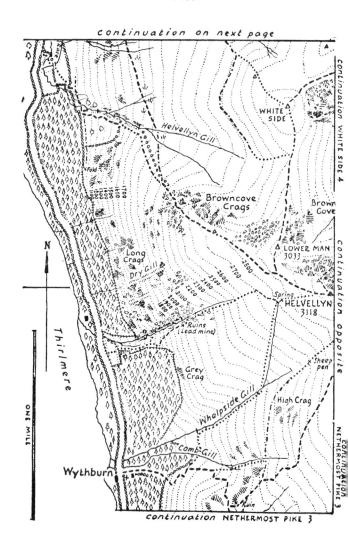

MAP

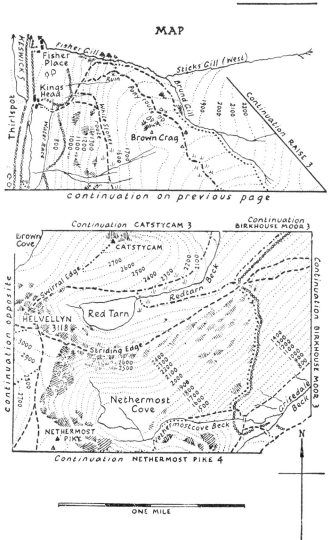

ONE MILE

THE WESTERN APPROACHES

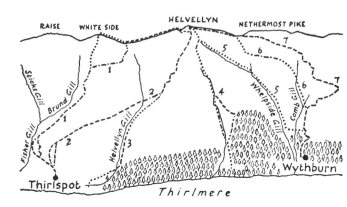

1 : **The old pony-route** : The original, longest and easiest route. The path is now becoming intermittent owing to disuse. This is the route indicated on the Ordnance Survey and Bartholomew's maps, but it is unnecessary to pass over the summit of White Side.

2 : **The 'White Stones' route** : The usual and popular way up from Thirlspot, originally marked by whitewashed stones (now a dim grey). Steep initially and midway, and marshy in places. Inexplicably this path, although long in use, is not shown on the published maps.

3 : **via Helvellyn Gill** : A more pleasant start to Route 2, but it is unremittingly steep for 2,000 feet. Dry underfoot. The correct start from the road is doubtful, and possibly involves a mild trespass: aim for the bridge in the field (over the water-race) and the plantation wall.

4 : **via the old lead mine** : The shortest way to the top from the road, taking advantage of a breach in the plantation. Very steep and rough for 2,200 feet. This is *not* a recognised route, and is not attractive. Solitary walkers with weak ankles should avoid it.

5 : **via Whelpside Gill** : A good route on a hot day, with water close almost to the summit. Rough scrambling in the gill. No path

6 : **via Comb Gill** : A route of escape from the crowds on the popular Birk Side path. Steep up by the gill, but generally easy walking most of the way, on grass. No path, but a shepherd's track is helpful if it can be found.

7 : **The 'Wythburn' route, via Birk Side** : One of the most popular ways up Helvellyn, and the usual route from Wythburn. Good path throughout. Steep for the first mile, then much easier. This is the route indicated on the published maps.

These routes are illustrated on pages 11 and 12 following

THE WESTERN APPROACHES

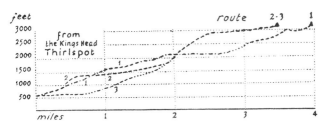

feet
route 2·3   1

from
the Kings Head
Thirlspot

3000
2500
2000
1500
1000
500

miles   1   2   3   4

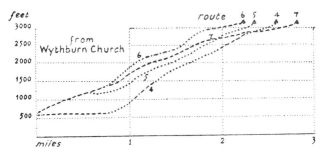

feet
route 6 5   4 7

from
Wythburn Church

3000
2500
2000
1500
1000
500

miles   1   2   3

Helvellyn Gill

In mist:

Route 1 is very difficult
    to follow.
Route 2 is fairly clear,
    but the divergences from
    Route 1 at 900' and 1000'
    are not distinct.
Route 3 is safe but is not
    easy to locate.
Route 4 is safe but seems
    even rougher in mist
Route 5 is safe if the gill
    is kept alongside.
Route 6 is better avoided
Route 7 is the best of all,
    the path being distinct
    throughout its length.

Whelpside Gill

ASCENT FROM THIRLSPOT
2600 feet of ascent: 3½ - 4 miles

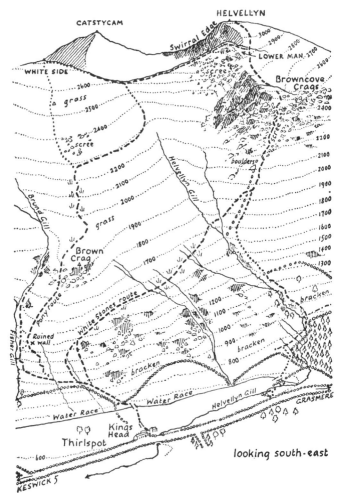

looking south-east

See Helvellyn 9 *for details of the routes illustrated*

ASCENT FROM WYTHBURN
2550 feet of ascent : 2¼ - 2¾ miles

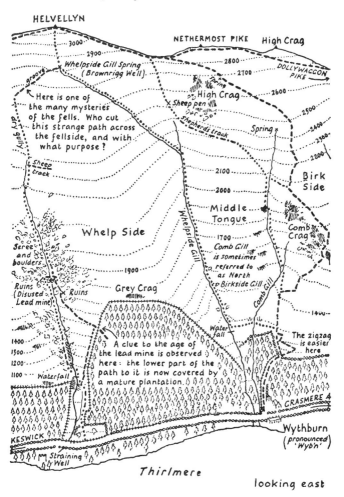

HELVELLYN

NETHERMOST PIKE   High Crag

3000

2900

Whelpside Gill Spring
(Brownrigg Well)

2800

DOLLYWAGGON PIKE

2700

← Here is one of
the many mysteries
of the fells. Who cut
this strange path across
the fellside, and with
what purpose ?

Spring

High Crag

✗ *Sheep pen*

Shepherds track

2600

2500

2400

2300

2200

Spring

Sheep crack

2100

Birk Side

2000

Middle Tongue

Comb Crag

Whelpside Gill

Whelp Side

1700
Comb Gill
is sometimes
referred to
as North
or Birkside Gill

Scree and boulders

1900

Grey Crag

Comb Gill

Ruins
(Disused
Lead mine)

Ruins

1400

Water fall

The zigzag
is easier
here

1400
1300
1200
1100

Waterfall

A clue to the age of
the lead mine is observed
here : the lower part of the
path to it is now covered by
a mature plantation.

CRASMERE 4

Wythburn
(pronounced)
'Wyb'n'

KESWICK

*Straining
Well*

Thirlmere

looking east

See Helvellyn 9 for details of the routes illustrated

THE EASTERN APPROACHES

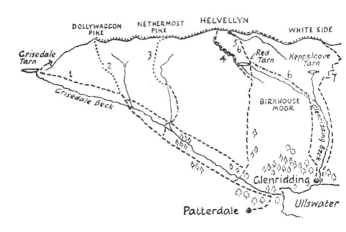

1 : *via Grisedale Tarn :* A long easy walk on a good path, with only one steep section. An interesting and pleasant route, which can be improved by following the edge of the escarpment between Dollywaggon Pike and the summit, instead of the path.

2 : *via Ruthwaite Cove and Dollywaggon Pike :* A very fine route for the more adventurous walker, cutting off a big corner of Route 1 — but the variation is steep and pathless.

3 : *via Nethermost Cove and Nethermost Pike :* A twin to Route 2, with a steep enjoyable scramble. Not for novices.

4 : *via Striding Edge :* The best way of all, well known, popular, and often densely populated in summer. The big attraction is an airy rock ridge, very fine indeed. Good path throughout.

5 : *via Red Tarn and Swirral Edge, from Patterdale :* An easier variation finish to Route 4, marshy by Red Tarn, ending in a good scramble up a steep rock staircase.

6 : *via Red Tarn and Swirral Edge, from Glenridding :* An easy walk, marshy in places, finishing with a good scramble up a steep rock staircase. Path intermittent but not difficult to follow.

7 : The old pony-route *via Keppel Cove :* The original route from Glenridding, now little-frequented but still quite distinct. A long but easy and interesting walk.

*Routes 4 to 7 are illustrated on pages 15 and 16 following.
For routes 1, 2 and 3, the diagrams on Dollywaggon Pike 5
and 7 and Nethermost Pike 6 respectively, will be helpful.*

THE EASTERN APPROACHES

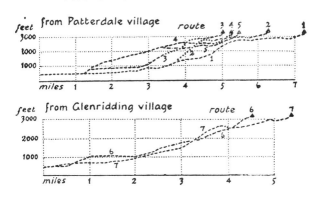

from Patterdale village — route 3 4 5 2 1

feet 3000 / 2000 / 1000 / miles 1 2 3 4 5 6 7

from Glenridding village — route 6 7

feet 3000 / 2000 / 1000 / miles 1 2 3 4 5

In mist :

Route 1 is easy to follow every inch of the way.

Routes 2 and 3 should be avoided absolutely.

Route 4 is safe for anyone already familiar with it.

Route 5 is safe, but there will be uncertainty near Red Tarn.

Route 6 is safe if Redtarn Beck is kept alongside to the tarn.

Route 7 is distinct except on the short south slope of White Side.

The summit, from Striding Edge

ASCENT FROM PATTERDALE
2700 feet of ascent : 5 miles

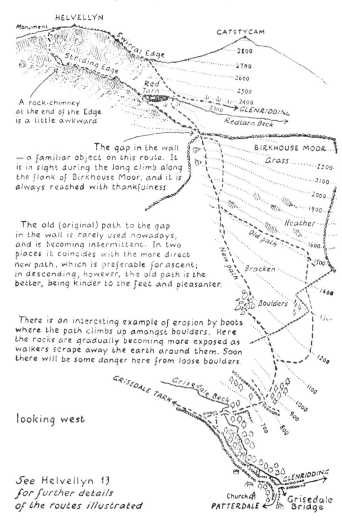

HELVELLYN

Monument

CATSTYCAM

Striding Edge

Swirral Edge

2800
2700
2600
2500
Red Tarn
2400
2300 GLENRIDDING

A rock-chimney
at the end of the Edge
is a little awkward

Redtarn Beck

The gap in the wall
— a familiar object on this route. It
is in sight during the long climb along
the flank of Birkhouse Moor, and it is
always reached with thankfulness.

BIRKHOUSE MOOR
Grass
2200
2100
2000
1900

The old (original) path to the gap
in the wall is rarely used nowadays,
and is becoming intermittent. In two
places it coincides with the more direct
new path, which is preferable for ascent;
in descending, however, the old path is the
better, being kinder to the feet and pleasanter.

Heather

Old path

1800

New path

1700

Bracken

1600

1500

1400

There is an interesting example of erosion by boots
where the path climbs up amongst boulders. Here
the rocks are gradually becoming more exposed as
walkers scrape away the earth around them. Soon
there will be some danger here from loose boulders.

Boulders

1300

1200

GRISEDALE TARN

Grisedale Beck

1100

looking west

1000

900

800

700

GRISEDALE
Church
PATTERDALE
Grisedale
Bridge

GLENRIDDING

See Helvellyn 13
for further details
of the routes illustrated

ASCENT FROM GLENRIDDING
2750 feet of ascent : 4½ or 5½ miles

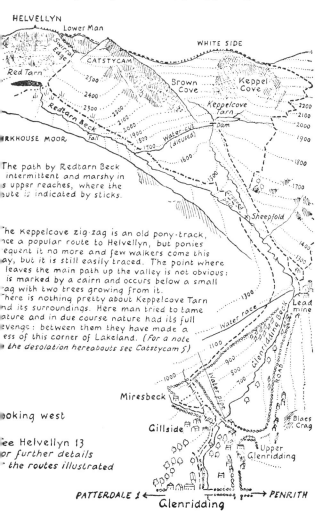

HELVELLYN

Lower Man

WHITE SIDE

Striding Edge

CATSTYCAM

2500

Red Tarn

2400

Brown Cove

Keppel Cove

2300

2200

Keppelcove Tarn

2200

2100

Redtarn Beck

2100

2000

Dam

2000

1900

1800

1700

RKHOUSE MOOR

Fall

Water-cut (disused)

1600

1900

1800

1500

1700

Sheepfold

1400

The path by Redtarn Beck
intermittent and marshy in
s upper reaches, where the
ute is indicated by sticks.

1300

1700

he Keppelcove zig-zag is an old pony-track,
ce a popular route to Helvellyn, but ponies
equent it no more and few walkers come this
ay, but it is still easily traced. The point where
leaves the main path up the valley is not obvious:
is marked by a cairn and occurs below a small
ag with two trees growing from it.
here is nothing pretty about Keppelcove Tarn
nd its surroundings. Here man tried to tame
ature and in due course nature had its full
evenge: between them they have made a
ess of this corner of Lakeland. (For a note
the desolation hereabouts see Catstycam 5)

1700

Lead mine

Water race

Glenridding Beck

1100

900

800

1000

700

Miresbeck

Water pipe

oking west

Gillside

Blaes Crag

ee Helvellyn 13
or further details
the routes illustrated

Upper Glenridding

PATTERDALE 1 ←   → PENRITH
Glenridding

ASCENT FROM GRASMERE
3050 feet of ascent : 6½ miles from Grasmere Church

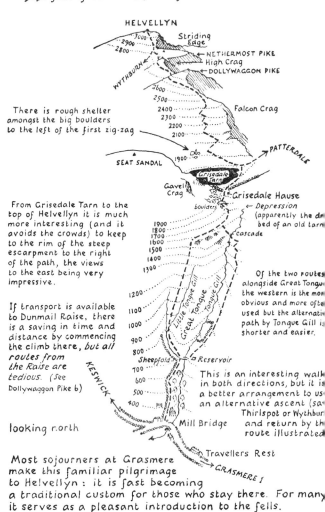

HELVELLYN

Striding Edge
← NETHERMOST PIKE
High Crag
← DOLLYWAGGON PIKE

Falcon Crag

SEAT SANDAL

Grisedale Tarn

Gavel Crag

Grisedale Hause

boulders

← Depression
(apparently the dry
bed of an old tarn

cascade

Lille Tongue Gill
Great Tongue
Tongue Gill

Sheepfold

Reservoir

KESWICK

Mill Bridge

Travellers Rest

→ GRASMERE 1

There is rough shelter amongst the big boulders to the left of the first zig-zag

From Grisedale Tarn to the top of Helvellyn it is much more interesting (and it avoids the crowds) to keep to the rim of the steep escarpment to the right of the path, the views to the east being very impressive.

If transport is available to Dunmail Raise, there is a saving in time and distance by commencing the climb there, but all routes from the Raise are tedious. (See Dollywaggon Pike b)

looking north

Of the two routes alongside Great Tongue the western is the more obvious and more often used but the alternative path by Tongue Gill is shorter and easier.

This is an interesting walk in both directions, but it is a better arrangement to use an alternative ascent (say Thirlspot or Wythburn and return by the route illustrated

Most sojourners at Grasmere make this familiar pilgrimage to Helvellyn : it is fast becoming a traditional custom for those who stay there. For many it serves as a pleasant introduction to the fells.

Helvellyn Lower Man

looking northwest

Helvellyn Lower Man, half a mile northwest of the principal top, occupies a key position on the main ridge, which here changes its direction subtly and unobtrusively. Walkers intending to follow the ridge north may easily go astray hereabouts. The wide path from Helvellyn skirts the Lower Man and continues clearly along a broad spur which appears to be the main ridge, but is not (*this is the direct way to Thirlspot, not indicated on Bartholomews' and Ordnance Survey maps*); while, being indistinct, the bifurcation to the Lower Man may not be noticed, *will* not in mist.

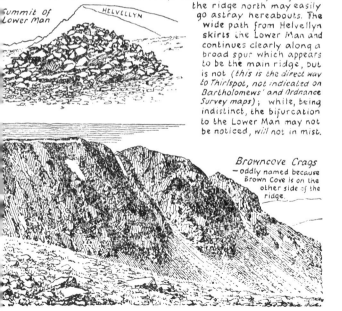

Summit of Lower Man

HELVELLYN

Browncove Crags
— oddly named because Brown Cove is on the other side of the ridge.

THE SUMMIT

It might be expected that the summit of so popular a mountain would be crowned with a cairn the size of a house, instead of which the only adornment is a small and insignificant heap of stones that commands no respect at all, untidily thrown together on the mound forming the highest point. It is a disappointment to have no cairn to recline against, and as there is no natural seat anywhere on the top visitors inevitably drift into the nearby wall-shelter and there rest ankle-deep in the debris of countless packed lunches. The summit is covered in shale and is lacking in natural features, a deficiency which man has attempted to remedy by erecting thereon, as well as the shelter, a triangulation column and two monuments. And until many walkers learn better manners there is a crying need for an incinerator also, to dispose of the decaying heaps of litter they leave behind to greet those who follow.

The paths across the summit are wide and so well-trodden as to appear almost metalled: they are unnecessarily and amply cairned.

The dull surroundings are relieved by the exciting view down the escarpment to Red Tarn and Striding Edge below.

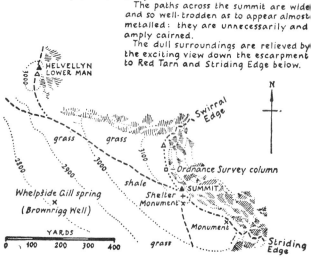

DESCENTS

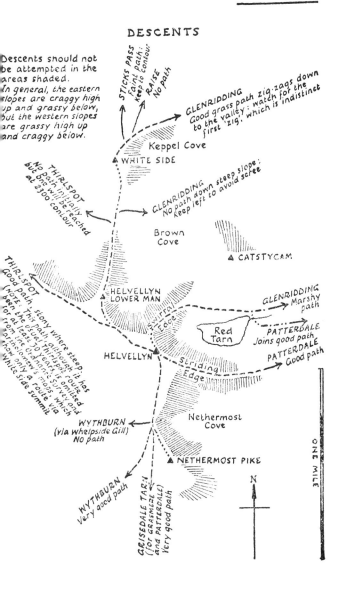

Descents should not be attempted in the areas shaded.
In general, the eastern slopes are craggy high up and grassy below, but the western slopes are grassy high up and craggy below.

STICKS PASS
Faint path;
keep to contour

RAISE
No path

GLENRIDDING
Good grass path zig-zags down to the valley; watch for the first 'zig', which is indistinct

Keppel Cove

▲ WHITE SIDE

THIRLSPOT
No path initially but one will be reached at 2300 contour

GLENRIDDING
No path down steep slope; keep left to avoid scree

Brown Cove

▲ CATSTYCAM

THIRLSPOT
Good path, stony where steep; it has been the usual Thirlspot route for at least 30 years. (NOTE: This path, although it has been omitted from the Ordnance Survey and Bartholomew's maps, which now show only a White Side route via the White Side summit.)

HELVELLYN LOWER MAN

Swirral Edge

GLENRIDDING
Marshy path

Red Tarn

PATTERDALE
Joins good path

HELVELLYN ▲

Striding Edge

PATTERDALE
Good path

WYTHBURN
(via Whelpside Gill)
No path

Nethermost Cove

WYTHBURN
Very good path

▲ NETHERMOST PIKE

GRISEDALE TARN
(for GRASMERE and PATTERDALE)
Very good path

N

ONE MILE

RIDGE ROUTES

To HELVELLYN LOWER MAN. 3033' : ½ mile : NW

Depression at 2975' 60 feet of ascent

A simple stroll, safe in mist.

Take the Thirlspot path, forking right below the cone of Lower Man. Or, better, follow the edge of the escarpment all the way.

NOTE : Helvellyn Lower Man stands at the point where the main ridge makes an abrupt and unexpected right-angled turn. Its summit must be traversed for White Side, Sticks Pass or Glenridding.

To CATSTYCAM, 2917' : 1 mile : NW (200 yards), then NE

Depression at 2600' 320 feet of ascent

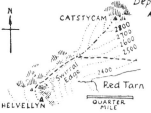

A splendid walk with a fine rock scramble. Safe in mist; dangerous in ice and snow.

200 yards north-west of the top of Helvellyn is a cairn (the Ordnance Survey column is midway), and just beyond, over the rim, is the start of the steep rock stairway going down to Swirral Edge : the descent is less formidable than it looks. Midway along the Edge the path turns off to the right : here continue ahead up the grass slope to the summit.

The Monuments of Helvellyn —

The Gough Memorial

Erected 1890 on the edge of the summit above the path to Striding Edge.

This small stone tablet, 40 yards S of the shelter, commemorates the landing of an aeroplane in 1926. (Playful pedestrians may have hidden it with stones)

The Dixon Memorial 1858

Situated on a platform of rock on Striding Edge overlooking Nethermost Cove (often not noticed)

RIDGE ROUTES

To BIRKHOUSE MOOR, 2350'. 2 miles : ESE then NE.
Minor depressions only : 100 feet of ascent

An unpleasant descent on loose scree, followed by an exhilarating scramble along a narrow rock ridge and an easy walk. Dangerous in snow and ice; care necessary in gusty wind; safe in mist.

Turn down the scree for Striding Edge 30 yards beyond the monument. The Edge begins with a 20' chimney, well furnished with holds; this is the only difficulty. From the rock tower at the far end the path slants across the slope but it is pleasanter to follow the crest.

BIRKHOUSE MOOR
Highest point.
PATTERDALE
HELVELLYN
Monument
Striding Edge
HALF A MILE

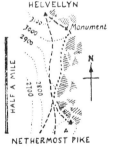

To NETHERMOST PIKE, 2920'
¾ mile : S then SE
Depression at 2840': 80 feet of ascent
A very easy walk. Safe in mist.

A broad path leads south to the depression. Here note, *in mist*, that the first few yards of the fork on to Nethermost Pike are not clear: the main path goes on to Wythburn and the unwary walker will go with it. A detour from the track across the flat top of Nethermost Pike is necessary to visit the summit cairn.

In clear weather a more interesting route follows the edge of the escarpment, the views being very impressive.

HELVELLYN
Monument
NETHERMOST PIKE
HALF A MILE

Whelpside Gill Spring
(Brownrigg Well)

Few visitors to Helvellyn know of this spring (the source of Whelpside Gill), which offers unfailing supplies of icy water. To find it, walk 500 yards south of west from the top in the direction of Pillar.

THE VIEW

The figures following the names of fells
indicate distances in miles

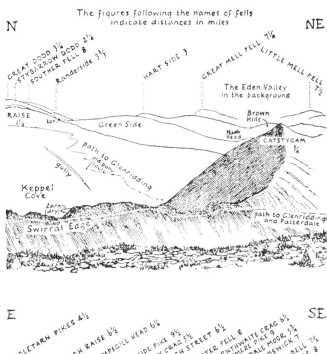

N — NE

GREAT DODD 3¼
STYBARROW DODD 2½
SOUTHER FELL 8
Randerside 3⅔
HART SIDE 3
GREAT MELL FELL
LITTLE MELL FELL 7½
7¼
The Eden Valley
in the background

RAISE 1¼
Lor...
Green Side
Brown Hills
Nook Head
CATSTYCAM ¼

Path to Glenridding
old pony route
gully
Keppel Cove
tarn (dry)
Swirral Edge
path to Glenridding
and Patterdale

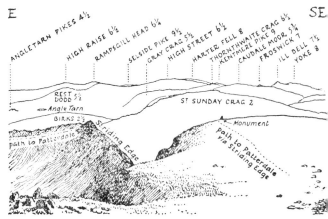

E — SE

ANGLETARN PIKES 4½
HIGH RAISE 6½
RAMPSGILL HEAD 6¼
SELSIDE PIKE 9½
GRAY CRAG 5½
HIGH STREET 6½
HARTER FELL 8
THORNTHWAITE CRAG 6½
KENTMERE PIKE 9
CAUDALE MOOR 5¼
FROSWICK 7
ILL BELL 7
YOKE 8

REST DODD 5½
Angle Tarn
BIRKS 2⅓
St SUNDAY CRAG 2
Monument
path to Patterdale
Striding Edge
path to Patterdale
via Striding Edge

THE VIEW

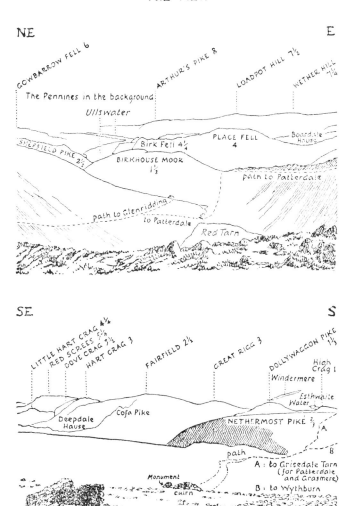

continued

THE VIEW

continued

S

SW

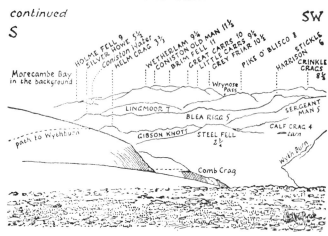

HOLME FELL 9
SILVER HOWE 5½
Coniston Water
HELM CRAG 3⅓

WETHERLAM 9½
CONISTON OLD MAN 11½
BRIM FELL 11
GREAT CARRS 10
LITTLE CARRS 9½
GREY FRIAR 10½

PIKE O' BLISCO 8

HARRISON
STICKLE
6

CRINKLE
CRAGS
8⅓

Morecambe Bay
in the background

Wrynose
Pass

SERGEANT
MAN 5

LINGMOOR 7

BLEA RIGG 5

CALF CRAG 4
cairn

path to Wythburn

GIBSON KNOTT

STEEL FELL
2¼

Wyth Burn

Comb Crag

W

NW

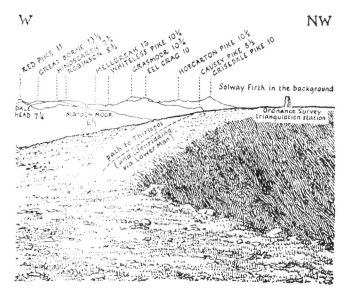

RED PIKE 11
GREAT BORNE 13½
HINDSCARTH 7½
ROBINSON 8½

MELLBREAK 12
WHITELESS PIKE 10½
GRASMOOR 10
EEL CRAG 10

HOBCARTON PIKE 10½
CAUSEY PIKE 8½
GRISEDALE PIKE 10

Solway Firth in the background

DALE
HEAD 7¼

MAIDEN MOOR
6½

Ordnance Survey
triangulation station

path to Thirlspot
(and Glenridding
via Lower Man)

THE VIEW

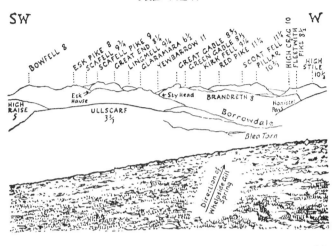

SW · W

BOWFELL 8
ESK PIKE 8
SCAFELL 9¾
SCAFELL PIKE 9
GREAT END 8½
LINGMELL 9½
GLARAMARA 6½
YEWBARROW 11
GREAT GABLE 8⅔
GREEN GABLE 8⅔
KIRK FELL 9½
RED PIKE 11½
SCOAT FELL 11½
PILLAR 10½
HIGH CRAG 10
FLEETWITH PIKE 8½
HIGH STILE 10½

HIGH RAISE 5
Esk Hause
ULLSCARF 3⅔
Sty Head
BRANDRETH 8
Honister Pass
Borrowdale
Blea Tarn

Direction of Whit' pside Gill Spring

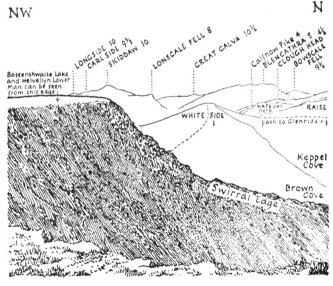

NW · N

LONGSIDE 10
CARL SIDE 9½
SKIDDAW 10
LONSCALE FELL 8
GREAT CALVA 10½
CALFHOW PIKE 4
BLENCATHRA 8
CLOUGH HEAD 4½
BOWSCALE FELL 9½

Bassenthwaite Lake and Helvellyn Lower Man can be seen from this edge.

WHITE SIDE 1
WATSON'S DODD
RAISE
path to Glenridding

Keppel Cove

Brown Cove

Swirral Edge

Heron Pike

2003'

from Grasmere

▲ FAIRFIELD

▲ GREAT RIGG

▲ STONE ARTHUR
▲ HERON PIKE
Grasmere ▲ NAB SCAR
• Rydal

Ambleside •

MILES
0   1   2   3   4

Heron Pike is a grassy mound on the long southern ridge of Fairfield. From no direction does it look like a pike or peak nor will herons be found there. It is a viewpoint of some merit but otherwise is of little interest. It is climbed not, as a rule, for any attraction of its own, but because it happens to lie on a popular route to Fairfield. The ridge beyond it undulates with little change of altitude before rising sharply to Great Rigg, and this hinterland of Heron Pike is generally referred to as Rydal Fell: for convenience it will be described in this chapter as a part of Heron Pike.

NATURAL FEATURES

Heron Pike is the watershed between Rydale and the
hort Greenhead valley. Grass predominates on its slopes
ut there is much bracken on the Rydale flank and rock
utcrops on both. Its streams are small and flow into
he Rothay. A dreary sheet of water named Alcock Tarn,
nce a reservoir, occupies a shelf above Grasmere; here
re many low crags. A nameless summit on the ridge
o the north of Heron Pike has a steep east face, which
at one point falls away abruptly in a formidable wall of
ock, Erne Crag (or Earing Crag), and, further north, the
ellside is cleft from top to bottom by a straight stony
ully, beyond which the ground becomes rough as Great
Rigg is approached. In contrast,
the western slopes adjoining
Great Rigg are entirely grassy.

Erne Crag

MAP

ONE MILE

continuation
GREAT RIGG 3

continuation
HART CRAG 3

continuation
STONE ARTHUR 2

continuation
NAB SCAR 2

Greenhead Gill

gully

Sheepfold

boulder

ruin

Erne
Crag

Blind
Cove

HERON
PIKE
2003

Rydal Beck

Swan
Hotel

AMBLESIDE

N

Alcock
Tarn

Lord
Crag

sheepfold

GRASMERE

plantation

RYDAL 1

1700 1800 1900
1700
1800
1900
300 400 500 600 700 800
300
400
500
600
700
800
1600
1500
1400
1300
1200
1000
1400
1300
1200
1100
1000 900

ASCENTS

Usually the summit of Heron Pike is visited only incidentally on the way to or from Fairfield, but it may be recommended as the objective of an easy and remunerative half-day's walk from Grasmere (via Alcock Tarn, to which there are three fair paths) or from Rydal (climbing Nab Scar en route). Gully-addicts will rejoice to learn that a long straight gully, full of shifting scree but with no difficulty other than steepness, falls from the ridge half a mile north of the summit, directly above the sheepfold in mid-Rydale beyond Erne Crag: this offers a scramble they (and they alone) will enjoy, but not even the most avid of them would find any pleasure in *descending* by this route.

THE SUMMIT

The summit is by a little outcrop of rock, distinguished by quartz. All else is grass. There is no cairn and nothing of interest except the view. The nameless north summit is better: at least it has a wall and cairn and a few rocks suitable for backrest.

DESCENTS: Any route of ascent (except the gully) may be used for descent. A quick way off to Rydal, in a season when the bracken is short, is by Blind Cove. *In mist*, keep *strictly* to the path going south to Nab Scar and Rydal.

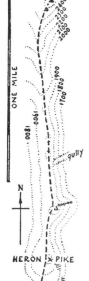

RIDGE ROUTES

To GREAT RIGG, 2513'
1½ miles : N then NNE
Minor depressions
550 feet of ascent
A pleasant high-level traverse

A good path undulates over grass and finally climbs the cone ahead. Safe in mist.

To NAB SCAR, 1450'
⅔ mile : S
Downhill all the way
A very easy descent

The path, on grass, forks at a cairn. Either branch may be taken — they soon join. Safe in mist.

THE VIEW

The smallness of the summit gives depth to the views, which are particularly rich in lakes and tarns. Nearby are the fells of the Fairfield Horseshoe, but the best of the mountain scene is formed by the finely-grouped Coniston and Langdale fells with Scafell Pike overtopping all.

rincipal Fells

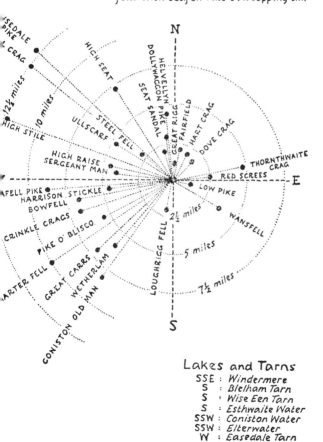

Lakes and Tarns

SSE	: Windermere
S	: Blelham Tarn
S	: Wise Een Tarn
S	: Esthwaite Water
SSW	: Coniston Water
SSW	: Elterwater
W	: Easedale Tarn

from Hartsop Beck

Patterdale

Hartsop

Hartsop
Hall

DOVE CRAG ▲ HIGH ▲ HARTSOP
DODD

LITTLE ▲
HART CRAG

RED ▲ SCREES

MILES

0   1   2   3

High Hartsop Dodd, seen from the valley near Brothers Water, has the appearance of an isolated mountain with a peaked summit and steep sides, a very shapely pyramid rising from green fields. But in fact it is merely the termination of a spur of a higher fell, Little Hart Crag, which it partly hides from view, and its uninteresting grassy summit has little distinction, though it is always greeted with enthusiasm by walkers who attain it direct from the valley, for the upper slopes above the sparsely-wooded lower flanks are excessively steep. A high ascending ridge links the Dodd with the rough top of Little Hart Crag.

MAP

Hartsop Beck is named Dovedale Beck on the 1" Ordnance Survey map

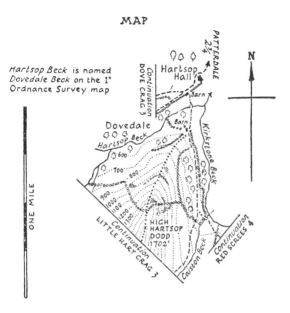

ASCENT FROM HARTSOP HALL
1200 feet of ascent

High Hartsop Dodd may be climbed direct from the barn at its foot — note here the symmetry between the pitch of the roof of the barn as it is approached across the boulder-dotted pastures from Hartsop Hall, and the sides of the pyramid of the Dodd behind — but the steepness of the grass slope, especially as the top wall is neared, makes the ascent laborious. It is really much better first to ascend Little Hart Crag (preferably by way of Dovedale) and to return to the valley over the top of the Dodd.

THE SUMMIT

There is no cairn to indicate the highest point — all is grass — and indeed it is not easy to say which is the summit; but it is assumed to be the top of the first rise above the wall.

This unassuming fell had its brief period of glory in 1948 when it won headlines in the newspapers by the efforts of rescuers to save two terriers trapped in a hole on the steep Caiston flank.

In descending, in mist, remember that the wall does not cross the ridge at right-angles, but at a tangent. Do NOT follow the wall down: on both flanks it leads to crags.

Dove Crag and Hogget Gill, from High Hartsop Dodd

THE VIEW

The most striking feature
in a moderate view is the
exceptionally fine picture
of Dovedale, which is seen
intimately in all its strong
and impressive contrasts.

Principal Fells

Lakes and Tarns
NNE: *Brothers Water*

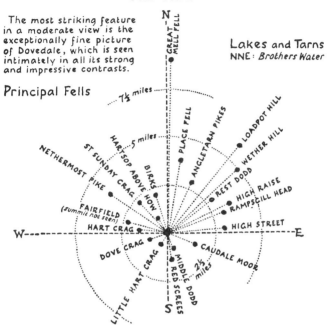

Brothers Water

High Pike

2155'

sometimes referred to as
Scandale Fell

from High Sweden Bridge

▲	DOVE CRAG
▲	HIGH PIKE
▲	LOW PIKE
●	Rydal
●	Ambleside

MILES
0   1   2   3

Everest enthusiasts will liken the two pronounced rises on the long southern spur of Dove Crag to the 'first and second steps' on the famous north-east ridge (but imagination would indeed have to be vivid to see in the grassy dome of Dove Crag any resemblance to the icy pyramid of that highest of all peaks!). The first rise is Low Pike, the second is High Pike. The latter, with its cairn perched on the brink of a shattered cliff, is the most imposing object seen from Scandale which lies far below.

Some authorities refer to High Pike as Scandale Fell, but the latter name is more properly applied in a general way to the whole of the high ground enclosing Scandale Bottom to north and west.

NATURAL FEATURES

Viewed from the south, High Pike has the appearance of an isolated peak; viewed from the parallel ridges to east and west, it is seen in its true proportions as merely the flat top of a rise in Dove Crag's long southern ridge; viewed from the north, it is entirely insignificant. High Pike, therefore, cannot be regarded as having enough qualifications to make it a mountain in its own right. Its level top, however, marks a definite change in the character of the ridge, which is narrow and rocky below and broad and grassy above. The western flank of High Pike descends to Rydale in uninteresting slopes relieved by occasional outcrops of rock; the eastern face is much rougher and steeper, with an ill-defined stony shoulder going down into Scandale.

MAP

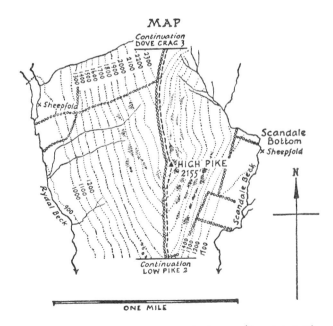

ONE MILE

NOTE: On Bartholomews 1" Map the summit is shown as 'Scandale Fell.'

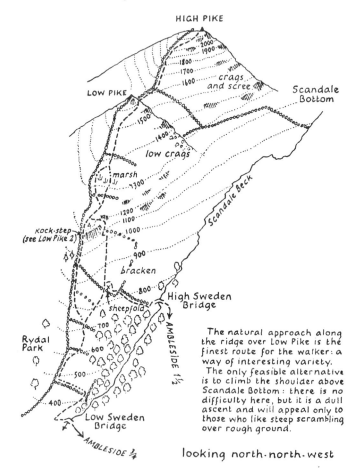

ASCENT FROM AMBLESIDE
2000 feet of ascent : 4 miles

HIGH PIKE

2000
1900
1800
1700
crags
and scree
1600
LOW PIKE
Scandale Bottom
1500
1400
low crags
marsh
1300
Scandale Beck
1200
1100
1000
Rock-step
(see Low Pike 2)
900
bracken
800
High Sweden Bridge
sheepfold
AMBLESIDE 1½
700
Rydal Park
600
500
400
Low Sweden Bridge
AMBLESIDE ¾

The natural approach along the ridge over Low Pike is the finest route for the walker: a way of interesting variety. The only feasible alternative is to climb the shoulder above Scandale Bottom: there is no difficulty here, but it is a dull ascent and will appeal only to those who like steep scrambling over rough ground.

looking north-north-west

This route, commonly used as the initial stage of the 'Fairfield Horseshoe', provides a pleasant walk along a good ridge. The lower approaches are very attractive.

THE SUMMIT

The summit is a flat grassy promenade with a cairn standing at the northern end on the edge of a decaying crag, overlooking Scandale. A high wall runs along the top.

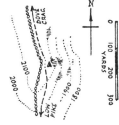

DESCENTS: The ridge-path should always be used when leaving the top: nothing but discomfort is to be gained by attempting a direct descent to east or west.

In bad weather conditions, a safe descent may be made to Ambleside by following the ridge over Low Pike, keeping to the path, or, if the path is lost, to the wall. A journey to Patterdale need not be abandoned in the event of bad weather on High Pike: the safe conclusion of the walk is ensured if the wall is followed north to a wire fence, which leads down grassy slopes to Dovedale or, alternatively, to Scandale Pass.

The wall

A traveller along the ridge cannot help but notice the wall: it accompanies him all the way and its intimacy becomes a nuisance. However, it is well worthy of notice, particularly on the steepest rises south of the summit, where the method and style of construction, in persevering horizontal courses despite the difficulties of the ground, compel admiration: it should be remembered, too, that all the stone had to be found on the fell and cut to shape on the site. Witness here a dying art!

RIDGE ROUTES

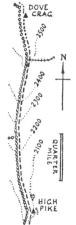

To DOVE CRAG, 2603' : 1 mile : N.
Slight depression : 470 feet of ascent

An easy, gradual climb on grass. Perfectly safe in mist.

Follow the wall north; an intermittent path keeps a few yards to the right of it. The cairn does not come into sight until a wire fence is reached.

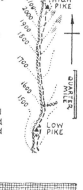

To LOW PIKE, 1657' : ⅔ mile : S.
Depression at 1575'
100 feet of ascent

An easy walk downhill on a rough but distinct path. Safe in mist.

The path keeps to the left of the wall and skirts the base of the top pyramid of Low Pike, the summit being attained by a short steep scramble.

from Scandale

THE VIEW

he ridge-wall obstructs the view westwards from the cairn
t is worth surmounting for the prospect of the Central Fells,
ich is good. In other directions, neighbouring higher fells
de the distance, but much of
e High Street range is seen
er the Scandale Pass.

rincipal Fells:

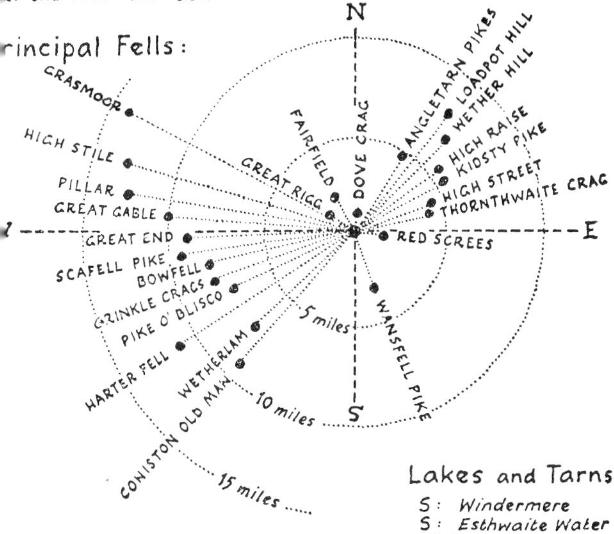

Lakes and Tarns:

S: Windermere
S: Esthwaite Water
SSW: Coniston Water

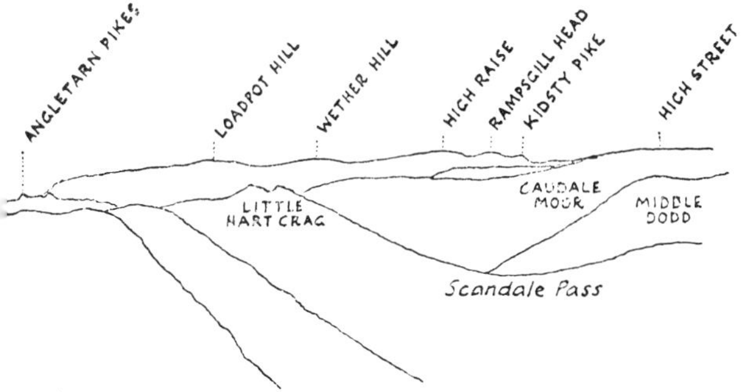

looking north-east

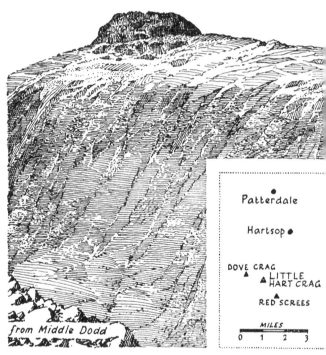

Patterdale

Hartsop •

DOVE CRAG
▲ LITTLE
▲ HART CRAG

▲ RED SCREES

MILES
0 1 2 3

from Middle Dodd

Little Hart Crag is the sentinel of Scandale Pass, four mile north of Ambleside, and takes its duty of guarding the Pas very seriously and proudly. It has the appearance, in fact, o a crouching watchdog, facing Scandale and missing nothing o the happenings there, while its spine curves down to the fields of Hartsop; the path from one place to the other climbs over it shoulder just beneath the hoary head and beetling brows.

It is really a very junior member in a company of grand hills and quite overshadowed by Red Screes and Dove Crag; but it ha individuality and an interesting double summit which command delightful views of Scandale and Dovedale.

NATURAL FEATURES

Little Hart Crag descends in uninteresting slopes of grass
and bracken to Scandale in the south; it is connected in
the west to Dove Crag by the broad marshy depression of
Bakestones Moss; south-east
is the lower depression of
Scandale Pass and the vast
soaring flank of Red Screes.
North-east is a narrow spur
running at a high elevation
before plunging sharply to
the valley at Hartsop: this

The summit, from the south

is High Hartsop Dodd, and its steep-sided pyramidal form,
seen from Brothers Water, gives it the appearance of being
a separate height. Just below the summit, west, is a long
wall of impressive crags, Black Brow. The eastern slopes,
falling to Caiston Glen, are rough and unattractive.

Hartsop, from the summit

MAP

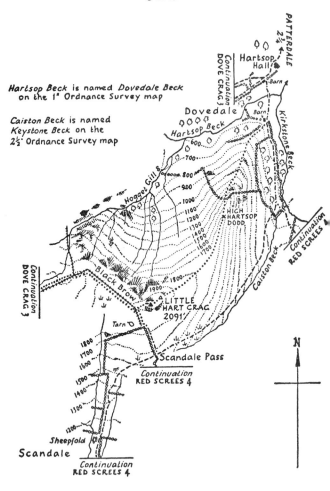

Hartsop Beck is named *Dovedale Beck* on the 1" Ordnance Survey map

Caiston Beck is named *Keystone Beck* on the 2½" Ordnance Survey map

ONE MILE

ASCENT FROM PATTERDALE
1,700 feet of ascent : 5 miles from Patterdale village

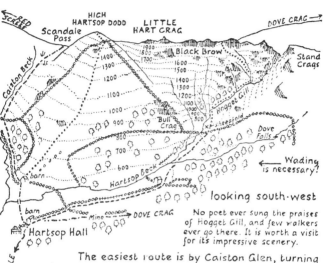

looking south-west

No poet ever sung the praises of Hogget Gill, and few walkers ever go there. It is worth a visit for its impressive scenery.

The easiest route is by Caiston Glen, turning right at Scandale Pass; the most interesting is via Hogget Gill, *which must not be attempted in mist.* The direct route over High Hartsop Dodd is steep.

ASCENT FROM AMBLESIDE
2,000 feet of ascent : 4¼ miles

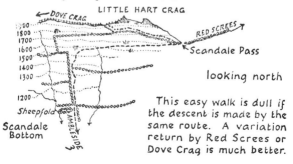

looking north

This easy walk is dull if the descent is made by the same route. A variation return by Red Screes or Dove Crag is much better.

THE SUMMIT

There are two well-defined tops. The higher is that nearer to
Dove Crag; it is surmounted by a cairn perched on the extreme
edge of a rocky platform. The lower summit, to the north-east, is
less conspicuous, but is easily identified in mist by markings of
quartz in the stones near the insignificant cairn: this cairn is
the key to the ridge going down to High Hartsop Dodd.   Both
summits are buttressed to the south by sheer walls of black rock.

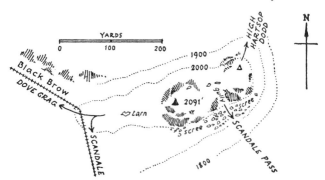

DESCENTS: The descent to Patterdale is best made directly
by the grassy ridge over High Hartsop Dodd, the last 1000 feet
down to the valley being steep. Scandale, for Ambleside, may
be reached by cutting off a corner at the top of the pass.
In mist, the summit is confusing and dangerous. The safest
way off is west to the wire fence, following this down south to
Scandale Pass for either Patterdale or Ambleside. Descents to
Caiston Glen or Dovedale direct should not be attempted.

THE VIEW

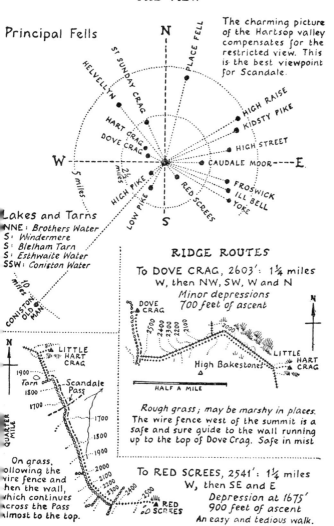

Principal Fells

N

PLACE FELL
HELVELLYN
ST SUNDAY CRAG
HART CRAG
DOVE CRAG
HIGH PIKE
LOW PIKE
RED SCREES

HIGH RAISE
KIDSTY PIKE
HIGH STREET
CAUDALE MOOR
FROSWICK
ILL BELL
YOKE

W

E

S

5 miles
2½ miles

The charming picture of the Hartsop valley compensates for the restricted view. This is the best viewpoint for Scandale.

Lakes and Tarns
NNE: Brothers Water
S: Windermere
S: Blelham Tarn
S: Esthwaite Water
SSW: Coniston Water

10 miles
CONISTON OLD MAN

RIDGE ROUTES

To DOVE CRAG, 2603': 1¼ miles
W, then NW, SW, W and N
Minor depressions
700 feet of ascent

N

DOVE CRAG
2500 2400 2300 2200 2100 2000
LITTLE HART CRAG
High Bakestones

HALF A MILE

Rough grass; may be marshy in places. The wire fence west of the summit is a safe and sure guide to the wall running up to the top of Dove Crag. Safe in mist

N

LITTLE HART CRAG
1900
Tarn 1800
1700
Scandale Pass
1700
1800
1900
2000
2100
2200
2300
2400
2500
RED SCREES

QUARTER MILE

On grass, following the wire fence and then the wall, which continues across the Pass almost to the top.

To RED SCREES, 2541': 1¼ miles
W, then SE and E
Depression at 1675'
900 feet of ascent
An easy and tedious walk.

Little Mell Fell

from Gowbarrow Fell

Little Mell Fell barely merits inclusion in this book. It *is* a fell — its name says so — but it is not the stuff of which the true fells are made. It rises on the verge of Lakeland but its characteristics are alien to Lakeland. It stands in isolation, not in the company of others. Its substance looks more akin to the sandstones of the nearby valley of Eden; its patchwork clothing, gorse and ling prominent, is unusual on the other fells; its hedges of stunted, windblown, unhappy trees and tumbledown fences are unsatisfactory substitutes for friendly stone walls. It is ringed by a quiet and pleasant countryside of green pastures and lush hedgerows, and one is as likely to meet a cow as a sheep on its slopes. There is good in all, however, and its heathery top is a fine place for viewing the (greater) merits of other fells.

◦ Penruddock

GREAT MELL FELL ▲

LITTLE ▲
MELL FELL

Pooley
Bridge ◦

◦ Watermillock
▲ GOWBARROW FELL
◦ Dockray

MILES
0   1   2   3   4

NATURAL FEATURES

Little Mell Fell is an outlier of the Helvellyn range and the last Lakeland fell in the north-east before the high country falls away to the wide plain stretching to the distant Border. It is an uninspiring, unattractive, bare and rounded hump — the sublime touch that made a wonderland of the district overlooked Little Mell — and few walkers halt their hurried entrance into the sanctuary to climb and explore it. In truth, there is little to explore. As though conscious of its failings it tries to aspire to normal mountain structure by throwing out two ridges, but the effort is weak and not convincing. One feels sorry for Little Mell Fell, as for all who are neglected and forlorn, but at least it is beloved of birds and animals and it is one of the few fells that grouse select for their habitat, and not even the great Helvellyn itself can make such a claim!

MAP

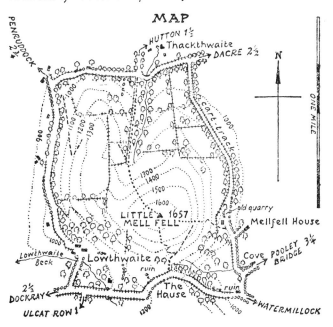

ASCENTS

The fell is almost entirely enclosed within fences and hedges but access may be gained at several places — from the Hause, from the cart-track just above Mellfell House, from the bridge near Thackthwaite, and by a green track from the road to the west — somewhat furtively, for there will be a doubt lurking in the mind of the climber as to whether he is committing an act of trespass.

It is difficult to plan a mountaineering expedition within a single square mile of territory, and probably it is best to climb straight up and down from the Hause and get the job done without frills : half an hour is sufficient from here. A better approach for the purist lies along the wooded hollow above the charming bridge near Thackthwaite : on this route the view is reserved as a last-minute surprise and comes as a reward for a dull climb.

THE SUMMIT

Unexpectedly there are some stones on the summit : these have been scraped together and formed into a low wall that may have been intended as a shelter or a shooting hide. An Ordnance Survey column is nearby. Heather covers the top.

DESCENTS : Descents may safely be made in any direction, in any weather, without the remotest risk of accident by falling over a crag; frisky bullocks are the only obstacles to be feared. The Hause, to which descents will be made usually, is not visible from the summit but comes into sight below by walking south, in the direction of Hallin Fell: beware rabbit-holes obscured by bracken on this slope.

Great Mell Fell from Little Mell Fell

THE VIEW

The diagram illustrates effectively the isolated situation of Little Mell Fell on the fringe of mountain country. One half of the view is of Lakeland, the other half of lowlands stretching away to the Pennines and the Border across the lovely Vale of Eden. This is one of the few good viewpoints for appreciating the shy beauty of Martindale. Gowbarrow Fell hides most of Ullswater, only the unexciting lower reach of the lake being in sight.

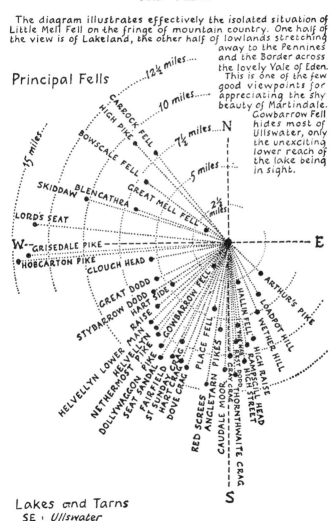

Principal Fells

Lakes and Tarns
SE : Ullswater

Low Pike

1657'

from Rydal Beck

▲ HIGH PIKE

▲ LOW PIKE

● Rydal

● Ambleside

MILES

0   1   2   3

Low Pike is well seen from the streets of Ambleside as the first prominent peak on the high ridge running northwards. The gradient along the crest of the ridge is slight, but Low Pike, halfway along, is sufficiently elevated above the deep valleys of Scandale, east, and Rydale, west, to give an impression of loftiness which exaggerates its modest altitude. There is a good deal of rock on the fell with several tiers of low crag. Low Pike is the objective in the fell-races at the annual sports meetings in Rydal Park.

MAP

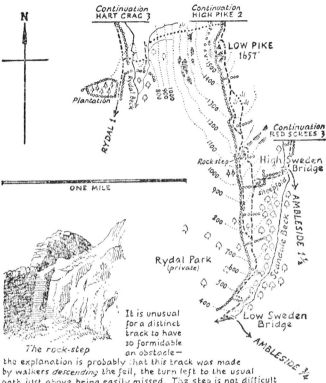

N

Continuation
HART CRAG 3

Continuation
HIGH PIKE 2

△ LOW PIKE
1657'

Plantation

RYDAL 1

Rydal Beck

1000
900
800

1500

1400

1300

1200

1100

△ Continuation
RED SCREES 3

Rock step

1000

High Sweden
Bridge

ONE MILE

900

sheepfold

AMBLESIDE 1½

800

Scandale Beck

700

Rydal Park
(private)

600

500

Low Sweden
Bridge

400

AMBLESIDE ¾

It is unusual
for a distinct
track to have
so formidable
an obstacle —

The rock-step

the explanation is probably that this track was made
by walkers *descending* the fell, the turn left to the usual
path just above being easily missed. The step is not difficult
to climb if the right foot is used first, the right foot in this case
being the left. There is no dignity in the proceeding, either up or down.

ASCENTS

Low Pike is invariably climbed from Ambleside, usually on
the way to the high fells beyond; it is, however, an excellent
objective for a short walk from that town. The approach, by
any of the variations, from the pleasant woods and pastures
to the bleak craggy ridge is very attractive. The wall along
the watershed detracts from the merits of this enjoyable walk.

Low Pike is invariably climbed from Ambleside, usually on
The climb from Rydal Beck is tedious; there is no path. Aged
pedestrians should note two hazards on this route: the crossing
of the beck first, and the scaling of the ridge-wall finally.

THE SUMMIT

The summit is an abrupt rocky peak, a place of grey boulders and small grassy platforms in the shadow of a substantial stone wall. Some of the rocks near the summit are big enough to afford simple practice in climbing. There is no cairn nor room for one: the wall occupies the highest inches.

DESCENTS: The way to Ambleside would be obvious even if there was no path. The point of divergence at 1200' is not clear: if the wall is followed beware the rock-step, which appears unexpectedly.

For Rydal, reverse the route of ascent. *In mist*, all descents should be made to Ambleside, keeping strictly to the path, or, if the path be lost, to the wall. There are crags at the 1200' level.

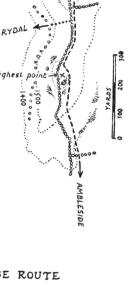

RIDGE ROUTE

To HIGH PIKE, 2155': ⅔ mile : N.
Depression at 1575': 600 feet of ascent.
A straightforward walk, safe in mist.
A distinct path follows the wall, climbing steadily most of the way amongst rocks.

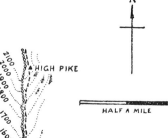

THE VIEW

All the attractiveness of the scene is centred between south and west, where the Coniston and Langdale fells rise grandly from a lowland of lakes.

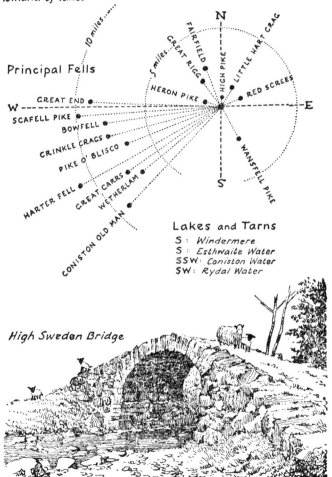

Principal Fells

10 miles
5 miles
N
FAIRFIELD
GREAT RIGG
HIGH PIKE
LITTLE HART CRAG
HERON PIKE
RED SCREES
W — — — — — — — — E
GREAT END
SCAFELL PIKE
BOWFELL
CRINKLE CRAGS
PIKE O' BLISCO
WANSFELL PIKE
HARTER FELL
GREAT CARRS
WETHERLAM
S
CONISTON OLD MAN

Lakes and Tarns
S : Windermere
S : Esthwaite Water
SSW : Coniston Water
SW : Rydal Water

High Sweden Bridge

Middle Dodd

from Caiston Glen

Patterdale

Hartsop

Hartsop
Hall

DOVE CRAG
MIDDLE DODD

RED SCREES

MILES
0   1   2   3

To the traveller starting the long climb
up to Kirkstone Pass from Brothers Water
the most striking object in a fine array
of mountain scenery is the steep pyramid
ahead: it towers high above the road like
a gigantic upturned boat, its keel touching
the sky, its sides barnacled and hoary.
This pyramid is Middle Dodd, the middle
one of three dodds which rise from the
pastures of Hartsop, all exhibiting the
same characteristics. When seen from
higher ground in the vicinity, however,
Middle Dodd loses its regal appearance
(as do the other two); its summit then
is obviously nothing more than a halt in
the long northern spur of Red Screes

MAP

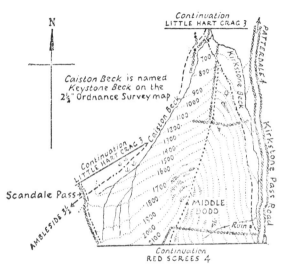

N

Caiston Beck is named
Keystone Beck on the
2½" Ordnance Survey map

Continuation
LITTLE HART CRAG 3

Kirkstone Beck

PATTERDALE 4

ONE MILE

Kirkstone Pass Road

Continuation
LITTLE HART CRAG 3

Caiston Beck

700
800
900
1000
1100
1200
1300
1400
1500
1600
1700
1800
1900
2000
2100

▲ MIDDLE
DODD

Scandale Pass

AMBLESIDE 3½

Ruin

Continuation
RED SCREES 4

ASCENT FROM HARTSOP HALL
1650 feet of ascent

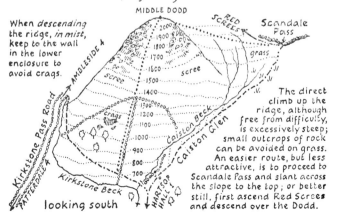

MIDDLE DODD

RED SCREES

Scandale
Pass

When descending
the ridge, in mist,
keep to the wall
in the lower
enclosure to
avoid crags.

AMBLESIDE 4

2000
1900
1800
1700
1600
1500
1400
1300
1200
1100
1000
900
800
700

scree

scree

grass

scree

Caiston Beck

Caiston Glen

Kirkstone Pass Road

PATTERDALE 4

crags

Kirkstone Beck

HARTSOP
HALL

looking south

The direct
climb up the
ridge, although
free from difficulty,
is excessively steep;
small outcrops of rock
can be avoided on grass.
An easier route, but less
attractive, is to proceed to
Scandale Pass and slant across
the slope to the top; or better
still, first ascend Red Screes
and descend over the Dodd.

THE SUMMIT

The top of Middle Dodd is a rather narrow grassy promenade. Its true altitude is slightly more than the 2106' attributed to it, for the ground immediately behind the rocky promontory which serves as the triangulation point rises gently to a knoll some twenty feet higher — here is the summit-cairn — before falling imperceptibly to the saddle linking Middle Dodd to Red Screes.

Near the cairn is a series of curious depressions like a line of sinkholes in limestone country, but as the rock here is volcanic the probability is that they are old earthworks; the detached boulders strewn about in them seem to suggest artificial excavation. Walkers who are neither archaeologists nor geologists will see in the depressions only a refuge from the wind.

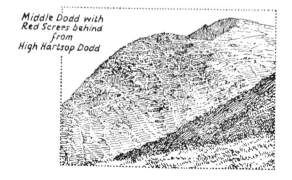

Middle Dodd with
Red Screes behind
from
High Hartsop Dodd

THE VIEW

Considering that Middle Dodd is hemmed in on all sides by higher fells, the view is remarkably good, and unexpectedly extensive in the south-west.

Principal Fells

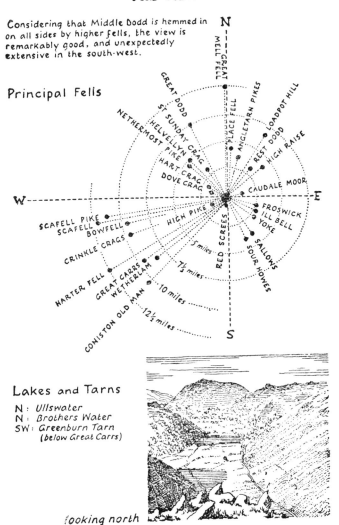

N

GREAT MELL FELL

GREAT DODD
ST SUNDAY CRAG
HELVELLYN
NETHERMOST PIKE
HART CRAG
DOVE CRAG
PLACE FELL
ANGLETARN PIKES
REST DODD
LOADPOT HILL
HIGH RAISE
CAUDALE MOOR

W — — — — E

SCAFELL PIKE
SCAFELL
BOWFELL
CRINKLE CRAGS
HIGH PIKE
FROSWICK
ILL BELL
YOKE
RED SCREES
SALLOWS
SOUR HOWES

HARTER FELL
GREAT CARRS
WETHERLAM
CONISTON OLD MAN

5 miles
7½ miles
10 miles
12½ miles

S

Lakes and Tarns

N: *Ullswater*
N: *Brothers Water*
SW: *Greenburn Tarn*
(below Great Carrs)

looking north

Nab Scar

1450'
approx.

▲ FAIRFIELD

▲ GREAT RIGG

▲ STONE ARTHUR

▲ HERON PIKE

Grasmere ▲ NAB SCAR
• ○ Rydal

Ambleside •

MILES
0 1 2 3 4

from Rydal Water

NATURAL FEATURES

Nab Scar is well known. Its associations with the Lake Poets who came to dwell at the foot of its steep wooded slopes have invested it with romance, and its commanding position overlooking Rydal Water brings it to the notice of the many visitors to that charming lake. It is a fine abrupt height, with a rough, craggy south face; on the flanks are easier slopes. Elevated ground continues beyond the summit and rises gently to Heron Pike. Nab Scar is not a separate fell, but is merely the butt of the long southern ridge of Fairfield.

MAP

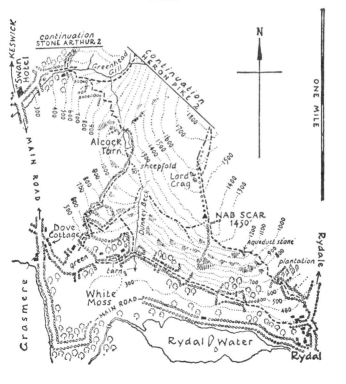

ASCENTS

The popular ascent is from Rydal, a charming climb along a good path, steep in its middle reaches; this is the beginning of the 'Fairfield Horseshoe' when it is walked clockwise. The path from Grasmere is much less used and is not easy to trace in its later stages but this is of no consequence in clear weather.

THE SUMMIT

Strictly, Nab Scar is the name of the craggy south face, not of the fell rising above it, but its recognised summit is a tall edifice of stones built well back from the edge of the cliffs, near a crumbled wall that runs north towards Heron Pike. Hereabouts the immediate surroundings are uninteresting, the redeeming feature being the fine view.

Nab Scar has a subterranean watercourse: below its surface the Thirlmere aqueduct runs through a tunnel. The scars of this operation are nearly gone, but evidence of the existence of the tunnel remains alongside the Rydal path, above the steepest part: here may be found a block of stone a yard square set in the ground; it bears no inscription but marks the position of the tunnel directly beneath.

HERON PIKE

1800
1700
1600
1500

HALF A MILE

Lord
Crag

1400

1300

N

NAB
SCAR

RIDGE ROUTE

To HERON PIKE, 2003': ⅔ mile: N
570 feet of ascent
An easy climb on grass
A plain path accompanies the old wall. When it forks, either track may be taken

THE VIEW

This is an 'unbalanced' view, most of it being exceptionally dull, the rest exceptionally charming. Lakes and tarns are a very special feature of the delightful prospect to south and west and the grouping of the Coniston and Langdale fells is quite attractive.

Principal Fells

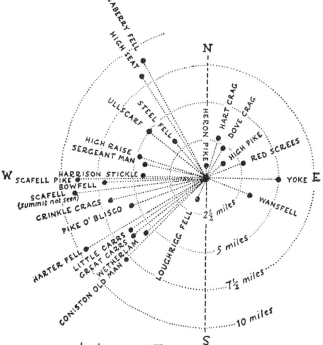

Lakes and Tarns

SSE : Windermere
S : Blelham Tarn
S : Esthwaite Water
SSW : Coniston Water
SW : Elterwater
WSW : Grasmere
WNW : Easedale Tarn
NW : Alcock Tarn

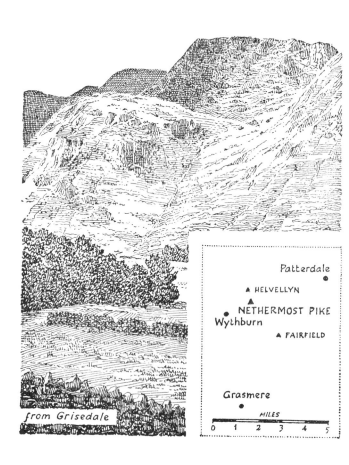

from Grisedale

Patterdale

▲ HELVELLYN

▲

● NETHERMOST PIKE

Wythburn

▲ FAIRFIELD

Grasmere
●

MILES

0   1   2   3   4   5

NATURAL FEATURES

Thousands of people cross the flat top of Nethermost Pike every year, and thousands more toil up its western slope. Yet their diaries record "climbed Helvellyn today." For Helvellyn is the great magnet that draws the crowds to Nethermost Pike: the latter is climbed incidentally, almost unknowingly, only because it is an obstacle in the route to its bigger neighbour. The grassy west slope trodden by the multitudes is of little interest, but the fell should not be judged accordingly: it is made of sterner stuff. From the east, Nethermost Pike is magnificent, hardly less so than Helvellyn and seeming more so because of its impressive surroundings. On this side a narrow rocky ridge bounded by forbidding crags falls steeply between twin hollows, deeply recessed, in a wild and lonely setting; here is solitude, for here few men walk. Here, too, is a gem of a tarn.

looking north

1	The summit of Nethermost Pike
2	High Crag
3	Ridge continuing to Helvellyn
4	Ridge continuing to Dollywaggon Pike
5	Comb Crag
6	Eagle Crag
7	Thirlmere
8	Whelpside Gill
9	Comb Gill
10	Birkside Gill
11	Nethermostcove Beck
12	Ruthwaite Beck
13	Grisedale Beck
14	Hard Tarn
15	Nethermost Cove
16	Ruthwaite Cove

The North Face

MAP

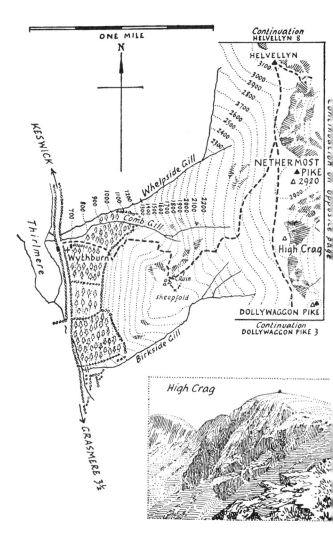

ONE MILE

N

KESWICK

Thirlmere

Whelpside Gill

Comb Gill

Wythburn

Birkside Gill

GRASMERE 3½

Continuation
HELVELLYN 8

HELVELLYN
3100

3000
2900
2800
2700
2600
2500
2400
2300

NETHERMOST
PIKE
△ 2920

2900

High Crag

DOLLYWAGGON PIKE

Continuation
DOLLYWAGGON PIKE 3

Continuation on opposite page

Ruin

sheepfold

High Crag

MAP

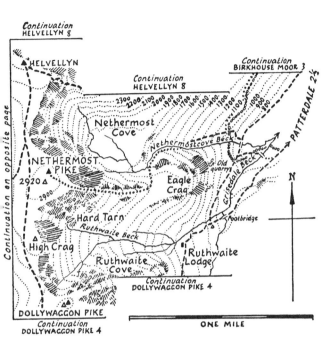

Continuation HELVELLYN 8

HELVELLYN

Continuation HELVELLYN 8

Continuation BIRKHOUSE MOOR 3

Nethermost Cove

Nethermostcove Beck

Continuation on opposite page

NETHERMOST PIKE

2920 △

2900

Old quarry

Eagle Crag

PATTERDALE 2½

Grisedale Beck

N

Hard Tarn

Ruthwaite Beck

High Crag

Footbridge

Ruthwaite Lodge

Ruthwaite Cove

Continuation DOLLYWAGGON PIKE 4

DOLLYWAGGON PIKE

Continuation DOLLYWAGGON PIKE 4

ONE MILE

Hard Tarn

ASCENT FROM WYTHBURN
2400 feet of ascent : 2 miles

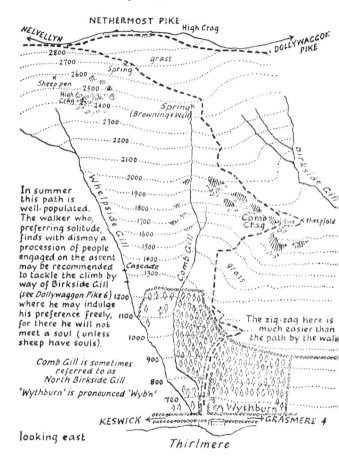

HELVELLYN

NETHERMOST PIKE   High Crag

DOLLYWAGGON PIKE

2800
2700   grass
Spring
2600
Sheep pen   2500
High   2400   Spring
Crag   (Browning's Well)
2300
2200
2100
2000
1900
1800   Comb
1700   Crag   sheepfold
1600
1500
Cascade 1400
1300
1200
1100   grass
1000

Whelpside Gill

Comb Gill

Birkside Gill

In summer
this path is
well-populated.
The walker who,
preferring solitude,
finds with dismay a
procession of people
engaged on the ascent
may be recommended
to tackle the climb by
way of Birkside Gill
(see Dollywaggon Pike 6)
where he may indulge
his preference freely,
for there he will not
meet a soul (unless
sheep have souls).

The zig-zag here is
much easier than
the path by the wall

Comb Gill is sometimes
referred to as
North Birkside Gill

900
800
700

'Wythburn' is pronounced 'Wyb'n'

KESWICK   Wythburn   GRASMERE 4

looking east   Thirlmere

The popular path to Helvellyn from Wythburn climbs
steeply up the side of Nethermost Pike, almost reaching
its summit before turning off to the higher fell: the top
is attained by a short detour. The path is very distinct.

ASCENT FROM GRISEDALE
2500 feet of ascent : 5 miles from Patterdale village

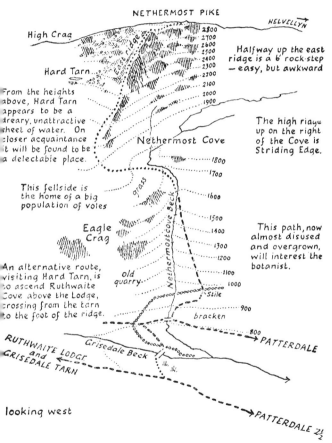

NETHERMOST PIKE

HELVELLYN

High Crag

Hard Tarn

Nethermost Cove

Eagle Crag

2800
2700
2600
2500
2400
2300
2200
2100
2000
1900

Halfway up the east ridge is a 6' rock-step — easy, but awkward

From the heights above, Hard Tarn appears to be a dreary, unattractive sheet of water. On closer acquaintance it will be found to be a delectable place.

This fellside is the home of a big population of voles

The high ridge up on the right of the Cove is Striding Edge.

1800
1700
1600
1500
1400
1300
1200
1100
1000
900
800

This path, now almost disused and overgrown, will interest the botanist.

An alternative route, visiting Hard Tarn, is to ascend Ruthwaite Cove above the Lodge, crossing from the tarn to the foot of the ridge.

old quarry

Nethermostcove Beck

Stile

bracken

PATTERDALE

RUTHWAITE LODGE and GRISEDALE TARN

Grisedale Beck

looking west

PATTERDALE 2½

This is a first-class route for scramblers, but staid walkers should avoid it and proceed *via* Grisedale Tarn. The east ridge is steep and exciting, finishing with an arête like a miniature Striding Edge. *This route should not be attempted in bad weather conditions.*

THE SUMMIT

The summit is of considerable extent and so remarkably flat that it is not easy to understand why the name 'Pike' was given to the fell (the top of the east ridge, however, has the appearance of a peak when seen from mid-Grisedale). It is mainly grassy — a field on top of a mountain — with thin flakes of rock around the cairn.

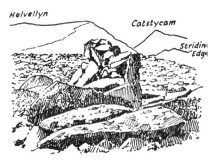

The broad top is level, and it is difficult to locate the highest point exactly, but the cairn illustrated appears to be slightly higher than the small ruined circular wall 100 yards southwes which has evidences of the former boundary fence and is ofte regarded as the top of the fell.

DESCENTS : A cairned path crosses the top but does not visi the actual summit. This path may be followed south to Grisedal Tarn for Grasmere or Patterdale. For Wythburn, cross this pat to another running lower along the fellside. The east ridge is quick way down to Patterdale, but is for experienced walkers on In bad weather conditions, leave the summit by one of the t paths mentioned : these are quite safe — the east ridge is no

RIDGE ROUTES

To HELVELLYN, 3118': ¾ mile : NW then N.

Depression at 2840' : 280 feet of ascent

An easy walk on a broad path, safe in mist.

The path west of the cairn on Nethermost
Pike continues north to Helvellyn, developing
into a wide uninteresting highway. It is far
better, in clear weather, to avoid the path
and follow the edge of the cliffs, the views
of Nethermost Cove and Striding Edge being
very impressive.

To DOLLYWAGGON PIKE, 2810'
1 mile : S then SE

Depression at 2700' : 120 feet of ascent

A very easy walk, safe in mist

The path west of the cairn on Nethermost
Pike continues south, skirting High Crag. It
crosses the breast of Dollywaggon Pike, the
summit of which is gained by a short detour.
(An inexperienced walker should not attempt
the detour in mist). A more interesting route,
in clear weather, is to follow the edge of the cliffs overlooking Hard
Tarn and Ruthwaite Cove, the rock-scenery being impressive.

Cascades in Birkside Gill

THE VIEW

Northwards, nearby Helvellyn shuts out the distant view, but in all other directions the panorama is very extensive. Nevertheless, the cairn is not a satisfactory viewpoint because the wide expanse of the summit-plateau occupies too much of the picture. A much more attractive and better-balanced view is obtained from the big cairn on High Crag to the south: from here the mountain scene is more pleasing, and additional lakes are visible, i.e. *Bassenthwaite Lake, Coniston Water, Esthwaite Water.*

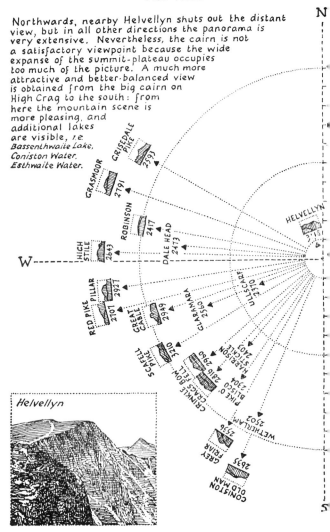

N

W

S

GRISEDALE PIKE 2593

GRASMOOR 2791

ROBINSON 2417

DALE HEAD 2473

HIGH STILE 2643

HELVELLYN 3118

RED PIKE 2707

PILLAR 2927

GREAT GABLE 2949

GLARAMARA 2560

SCAFELL PIKE 3210

ULLSCARF 2370

GRINDLE CRAGS 2560

BOW FELL 2960

PIKE O' BLISCO 2304

HARRISON STICKLE 2403

WETHERLAM 2502

GREY FRIAR 2536

CONISTON OLD MAN 2635

Helvellyn

THE VIEW

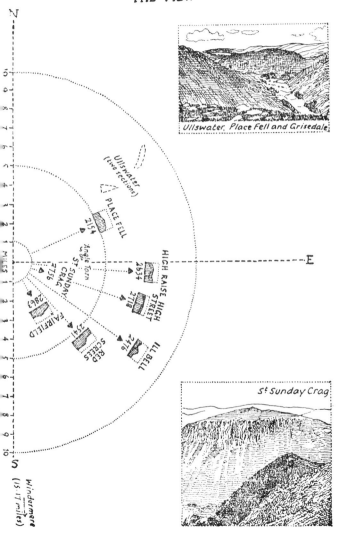

Ulswater, Place Fell and Grisedale

St Sunday Crag

N

10
9
8
7
6
5
4
3
2
1
MILES
1
2
3
4
5
6
7
8
9
10

E

S

Windermere (15 17 miles)

Ulswater (two sections)

PLACE FELL
2154

Angle Tarn

ST SUNDAY CRAG
2756

HIGH RAISE
2634

HIGH STREET
2718

FAIRFIELD
2863

RED SCREES
2541

ILL BELL
2476

Raise

2889'

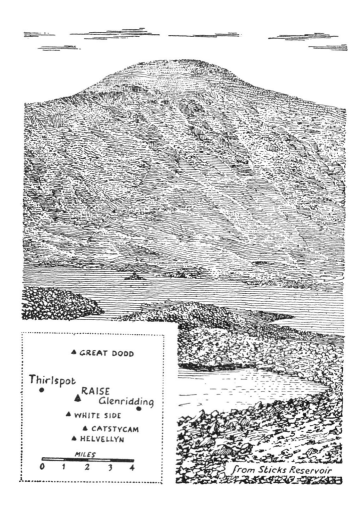

GREAT DODD ▲

Thirlspot
●

RAISE ▲
Glenridding
●

▲ WHITE SIDE

▲ CATSTYCAM
▲ HELVELLYN

MILES

0   1   2   3   4

from Sticks Reservoir

NATURAL FEATURES

Raise deserves a special cheer. It is the only summit in the Helvellyn range adorned with a crown of rough rocks — and they make a welcome change from the dull monotony of the green expanses around Sticks Pass. But in general the fell conforms to the usual Helvellyn pattern, the western slopes being grassy and the eastern slopes more scarred. It further differs from its fellows on the main ridge, however, in that its western slopes do not reach down to the valley: they are sandwiched between the more extensive, sprawling flanks of Stybarrow Dodd and White Side and are crowded out completely at the 1600' contour.

looking north

1: *The summit*
2: *Rock tor*
3: *Sticks Pass*
4: *Ridge continuing to White Side*
5: *Stang*
6: *Stang End*
7: *Keppel Cove*

8: *Keppelcove Tarn (dry)*
9: *Sticks Reservoir*
10: *Sticks Gill (East)*
11: *Sticks Gill (West)*
12: *Brund Gill*
13: *Glenridding Beck*
14: *Rowten Beck*

The Rock Tor

This small outcrop rises from a slope of lichened scree. It is not remarkable in itself, but stands out so prominently that it forms a ready means of identifying Raise in all views where the east slope is seen in profile.

MAP

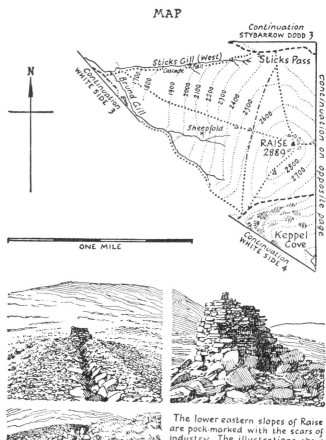

Continuation
STYBARROW DODD 3

Sticks Gill (West)   Sticks Pass

Cascade   Fall

Continuation
WHITE SIDE 3

Brund Gill

1700
1800
1900
2000
2100
2200
2300
2400
2500
2600
2700
2800

continuation on opposite page

Sheepfold

RAISE
2889

Continuation
WHITE SIDE 4

Keppel
Cove

N

ONE MILE

The lower eastern slopes of Raise
are pock-marked with the scars of
industry. The illustrations above
show the now-disused and derelict
chimney and stone aqueduct which
formerly served the Glenridding
lead mine. Only a small portion of
the aqueduct remains intact (see
picture on left) but it is sufficient
to indicate the skill of the masons
who built it and to make one envy
their pride in the job, and be glad
they are not here to see the ruins.

MAP

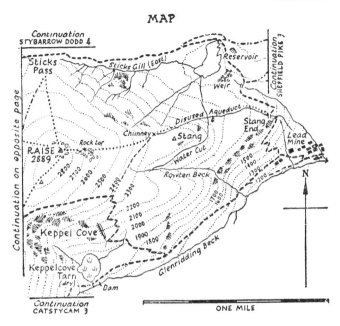

Continuation
STYBARROW DODD 4

Sticks Gill (East)

Reservoir

Continuation
SHEFFIELD PIKE 3

Sticks
Pass

Weir

Continuation on opposite page

Disused Aqueduct

Stang
End

Lead
Mine

Chimney

Stang

RAISE
2889

Rock Tor

2800 2700 2600 2500

Water Cut

1600 1500 1400 1300 1200

Rowten Beck

2400 2300

N

2200
2100

Keppel Cove

2000
1900 1800

Keppelcove
Tarn
(dry)

1700

Dam

Glenridding Beck

Continuation
CATSTYCAM 3

ONE MILE

Glenridding and Ullswater, from Stang End

ASCENTS FROM STANAH AND THIRLSPOT
2400 feet of ascent : 2½ miles

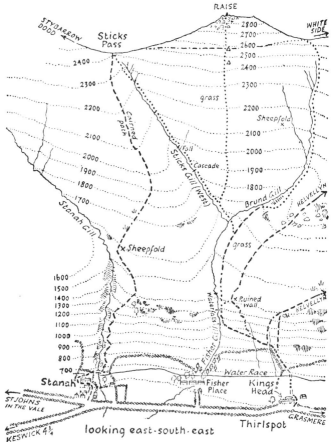

looking east-south-east

Raise overlooks Sticks Pass, from which it is climbed very easily; the path from Stanah to the top of the pass is therefore a convenient route of ascent. Routes from Thirlspot are more direct but lack paths much of the way. All the western approaches are grassy and rather dull.

ASCENT FROM GLENRIDDING
2500 feet of ascent : 4 miles from Glenridding village

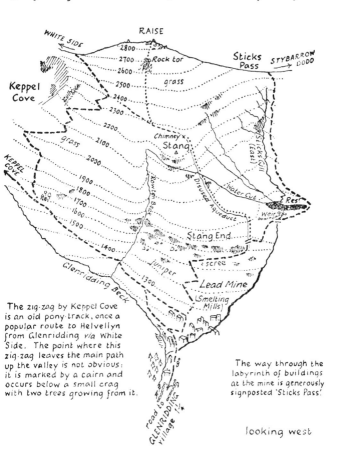

RAISE

WHITE SIDE

2800
2700 · · · Rock tor
2600
2500   grass
2400
2300
2200
grass   2100
2000
1900
1800
1700
1500
1400

Keppel Cove

KEPPEL COVE

Sticks Pass   STYBARROW DODD →

Chimney ×
Stang

Sticks Gill (east)

Water Cut
Disused Aqueduct

Res

Weir

Stang End

scree

Rowten Beck

Glenridding beck

Juniper
1300

Lead Mine
(Smelting Mills)

road to GLENRIDDING village 1½

The zig-zag by Keppel Cove is an old pony-track, once a popular route to Helvellyn from Glenridding via White Side. The point where this zig-zag leaves the main path up the valley is not obvious: it is marked by a cairn and occurs below a small crag with two trees growing from it.

The way through the labyrinth of buildings at the mine is generously signposted 'Sticks Pass'.

looking west

All routes from the east are marred by the inescapable evidences of the lead mine. The Keppel Cove route is easy, and gives impressive views of Catstycam. The approach by Sticks Pass is dull, that by the old aqueduct rather better.

THE SUMMIT

The summit is a level grassy plateau, capped at its higher end by an outcrop of very rough gnarled stones. Alongside the main cairn is an iron estate-boundary post. Smaller cairns on nearby rocks indicate other viewpoints. There are no paths.

DESCENTS: In good weather all routes of ascent are suitable also for descent. The quickest way to Thirlspot is down the western slope, joining a path by Fisher Gill. For Glenridding, the route by the old aqueduct is quickest; if the zig-zag by Keppel Cove is preferred, a big corner may be saved initially by descending to it south-east from the summit.
In bad conditions, head for the *top* of Sticks Pass, north, whatever the destination.
In mist, note that the boundary post is on the south-west side of the cairn.

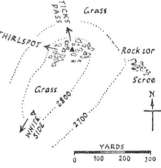

The summit of Stang

RIDGE ROUTES

To STYBARROW DODD, 2770' : 1 mile : N, then NE

Depression at 2420' (Sticks Pass)
350 feet of ascent

Grass all the way after initial stones. Easy.
No path, but safe in mist.

Cross Sticks Pass at its highest point, by a small tarn, and continue up the steepening slope opposite. The boundary stone reached first is usually accepted as the top of the Dodd, but there is higher ground beyond.

To WHITE SIDE, 2832' : ¾ mile : SW

Depression at 2650'. 200 feet of ascent.

Easy walking on grass. No path to the depression but safe in mist.

HALF A MILE

Cross the summit plateau to the south-west cairn and descend therefrom to the good path coming up on the left: it climbs easily to the top of White Side.

This slope is a favourite with skiers and, on snowy winter days, presents an animated scene : a ski-lift operates.

Raise from Sticks Pass

THE VIEW

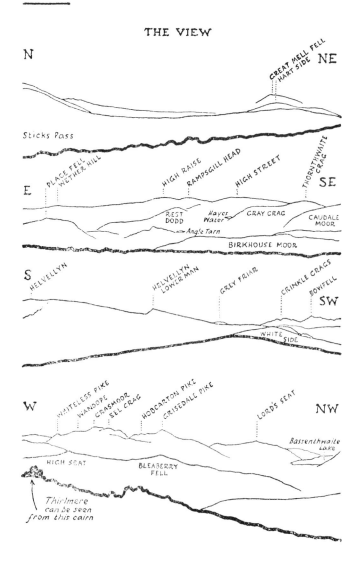

THE VIEW

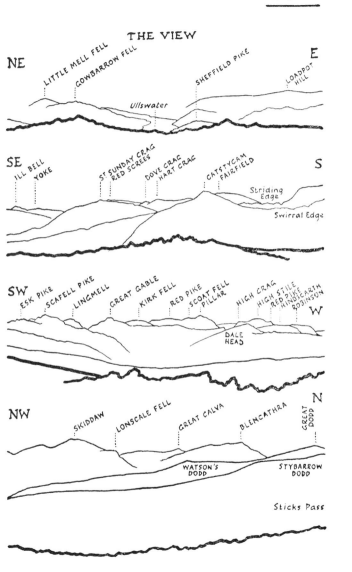

Red Screes

2541'

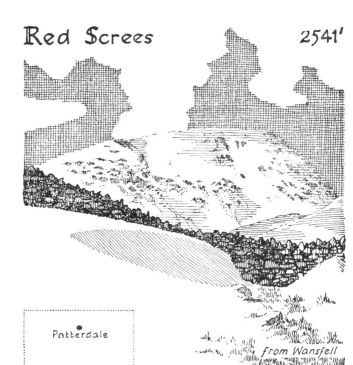

from Wansfell

Prominent in all views of the Lakeland fells from the lesser heights of South Westmorland is the high whale-backed mass of Red Screes, rising in a graceful curve from the head of Windermere and descending abruptly at its northern end. Some maps append the name 'Kilnshaw Chimney' to the summit, but Red Screes is its name by popular choice—**and Red Screes** it should be because of the colour and character of its eastern face. It is a friendly accommodating hill, holding no terrors for those who climb to its summit by the usual easy routes and being very conveniently situated for sojourners at Ambleside; moreover, it offers a reward of excellent views.

Patterdale

Hartsop ●

▲ DOVE CRAG

▲ RED SCREES

● Ambleside

MILES
0   1   2   3

NATURAL FEATURES

All travellers along the Kirkstone Pass are familiar with Red Screes, for it is the biggest thing to be seen there: for four miles it forms the western wall of the pass. In general structure it is a long broad ridge of considerable bulk. The southern slopes are at an easy gradient, with rock outcrops in abundance and a quarry which produces beautiful green stone; in places the rough ground steepens into crags. The shorter north ridge, after a gradual descent to the lesser height of Middle Dodd, plunges steeply to the fields of High Hartsop. The western slopes are of no particular interest and the pride of Red Screes is undoubtedly its eastern face, where natural forces have eroded two combes which carve deeply into the mountain on both flanks of a wide buttress: runs of fine red scree pour down these hollows. This side of the fell has many crags and tumbled boulders, one of which gave the pass its name; high up is Kilnshaw Chimney, which is hardly as significant as the maps would imply, being only a narrow gully choked with scree.

Red Screes, although in the midst of high country, contrives to appear more isolated from its fellows than any other of the eastern fells. It is independent and is unsupported, not buttressed by its neighbours: to this extent, it may be said to have the purest mountain form among the eastern fells.

Of the many streams which have their birth on Red Screes, the best-known is Stock Ghyll, flowing south and breaking in lovely waterfalls on its way to join the Rothay; on the west, innumerable watercourses feed Scandale Beck; northwards, Kirkstone Beck and Caiston Beck carry its waters to Ullswater.

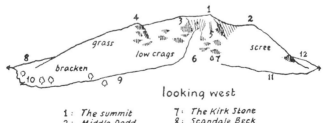

looking west

1: The summit	7: The Kirk Stone
2: Middle Dodd	8: Scandale Beck
3: Raven Crag	9: Stock Ghyll
4: Snarker Pike	10: Stock Ghyll Force
5: Kilnshaw Chimney	11: Kirkstone Beck
6: Kirkstone Pass	12: Caiston Beck

MAP

Continuation on opposite page

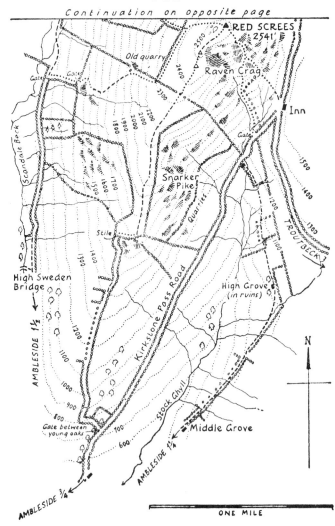

RED SCREES
2541'

Old quarry

Raven Crag

2500

2400

Gate   Gate

2300

Inn

2200

Scandale Beck

2100
2000
1900
1800

Gate

1700

1600

Snarker
Pike

1500

1500

1400

1300

Quarries

1500

Stile

1100

1200

TROUTBECK 3

1300
1400

High Sweden
Bridge

1300

Kirkstone Pass Road

High Grove
(in ruins)

AMBLESIDE 1½

1200

N

1100

1000

900

Stock Ghyll

800

Gate between
young oaks

700

Middle Grove

600

AMBLESIDE 1¼

AMBLESIDE ¾

ONE MILE

MAP

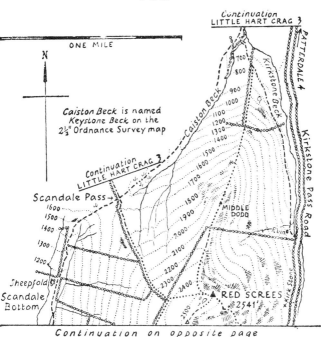

ONE MILE

N

Caiston Beck is named Keystone Beck on the 2½" Ordnance Survey map

Continuation LITTLE HART CRAG 3

PATTERDALE 4

Caiston Beck

Kirkstone Beck

Kirkstone Pass Road

700
800
900
1000
1100
1200
1300
1400
1500
1600
1700
1800
1900
2000
2100
2200
2300
2400

Continuation LITTLE HART CRAG 2

Scandale Pass →

1600
1500
1400
1300
1200

Sheepfold

Scandale Bottom

MIDDLE DODD

Ruin

Kirkstone

▲ RED SCREES
2541'

Continuation on opposite page

The Kirk Stone

This fallen boulder stands about sixty yards to the left (west) of the road at the top of the steep descent to the north. It is a prominent object on the way up the pass from Brothers Water, having the appearance of a ridged church-tower.

But the 2½" Ordnance Survey map suggests that the Kirk Stone is on the opposite side of the road: there are certainly many larger boulders here but none resembling a church.

ASCENT FROM AMBLESIDE
2400 feet of ascent : 4 or 5 miles

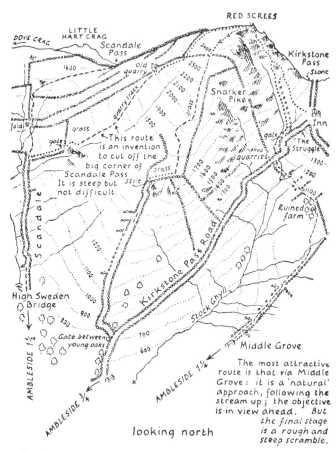

looking north

Of the routes shown, two only are commonly in use:
the direct ridge route (which is better in descending)
and the longer Scandale Pass route (the safest in bad
weather). The best 'round tour' is to ascend by Middle
Grove and return by descending the ridge.

ASCENT FROM PATTERDALE
2200 feet of ascent : 6½ miles from Patterdale village

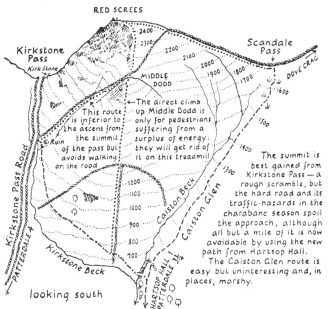

RED SCREES

Kirkstone Pass

Kirk Stone

Scandale Pass

DOVE CRAG

MIDDLE DODD

This route is inferior to the ascent from the summit of the pass but avoids walking on the road

Ruin

The direct climb up Middle Dodd is only for pedestrians suffering from a surplus of energy: they will get rid of it on this treadmill

Kirkstone Pass Road

PATTERDALE 4

Kirkstone Beck

Caiston Beck

Caiston Glen

The summit is best gained from Kirkstone Pass — a rough scramble, but the hard road and its traffic-hazards in the charabanc season spoil the approach, although all but a mile of it is now avoidable by using the new path from Hartsop Hall.

The Caiston Glen route is easy but uninteresting and, in places, marshy.

looking south

HARTSOP HALL 3½
PATTERDALE 3½

The approach from Patterdale is very fine, but a little road·walking, both going and returning, robs the journey of some of its charm; alternatives along the valley can be found, however. The popular route is by Caiston Glen.

looking down on the Kirkstone Pass Inn

THE SUMMIT

The summit is a large grassy plateau, having three principal cairns widely spaced and differing little in altitude. There is no mistaking the highest, a huge mound of stones situated at the extreme corner of the plateau: a dramatic site, for here the ground seems to collapse at one's feet and plunge steeply down to the winding road far below. An Ordnance Survey column stands alongside, and twenty yards west is a small tarn with a few satellite ponds nearby. Below and east of the highest cairn is a prominent cluster of rocks worth visiting: it is a good vantage point and a pleasant place to eat sandwiches if the top is crowded, but it is well to tread cautiously here: beware crag!

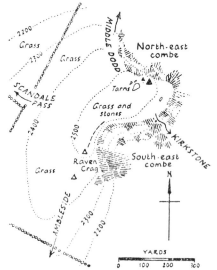

DESCENTS: The best way down to Ambleside is by the south ridge — it is so easy a saunter that the hands need be taken from the pockets only once, to negotiate a stile. Also easy, but longer, is the Scandale Pass route. The direct descent to Kirkstone is rough, too rough to be enjoyable.

For Patterdale, the way over Middle Dodd is excellent, but steep. The Caiston Glen path is easy, but descents to Kirkstone are not recommended, except for the *very* thirsty.

In bad weather, the safest course of all is to aim for the top of Scandale Pass — for either Ambleside or Patterdale.

Patterdale, from the summit

LITTLE HART CRAG

2000

1900
Tarn

Scandale
Pass

1800

1700

QUARTER MILE

1700

1800

1900

2000

2100

2200

2300

2400

RED SCREES

Red Screes
has no high
connecting link
with any other
major fell. On the
Fairfield round the
next adjacent fell
is Little Hart Crag

RIDGE ROUTE

To LITTLE HART CRAG, 2091': 1¼ miles
W, then NW and E

*Depression at 1675'
430 feet of ascent*

An easy and tedious walk.

On grass, following the wall
across Scandale Pass. Little
Hart Crag is not safe in mist

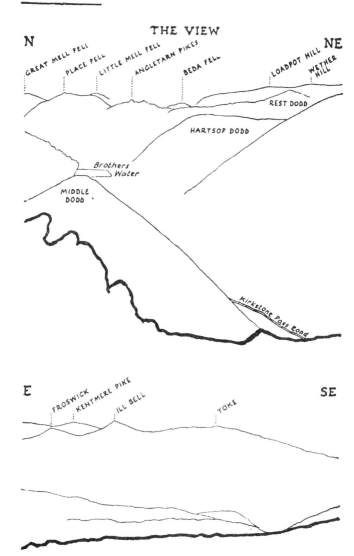

THE VIEW

N

NE

GREAT MELL FELL · PLACE FELL · LITTLE MELL FELL · ANGLETARN PIKES · BEDA FELL · LOADPOT HILL · WETHER HILL

REST DODD

HARTSOP DODD

Brothers Water

MIDDLE DODD

Kirkstone Pass Road

E

SE

FROSWICK · KENTMERE PIKE · ILL BELL · YOKE

THE VIEW

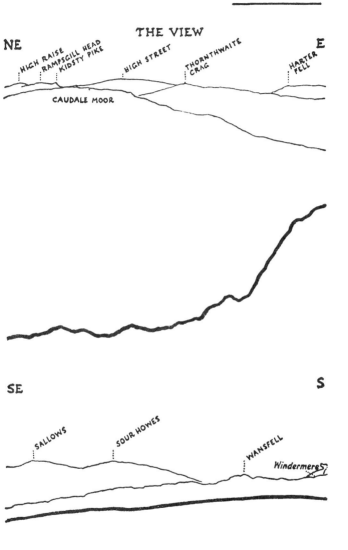

continued

THE VIEW

continued

S   SW

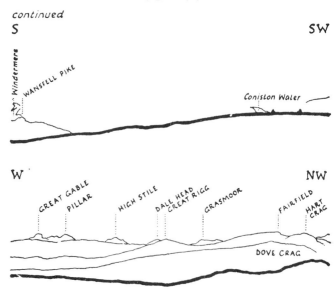

Windermere

WANSFELL PIKE

Coniston Water

W   NW

GREAT GABLE

PILLAR

HIGH STILE

DALE HEAD
GREAT RIGG

GRASMOOR

FAIRFIELD

HART
CRAG

DOVE CRAG

The south-east combe

The north-east combe

THE VIEW

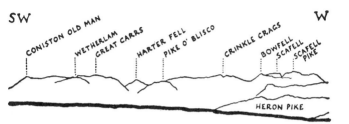

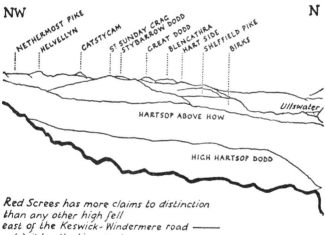

Red Screes has more claims to distinction
than any other high fell
east of the Keswick - Windermere road ——
   (a) it has the biggest cairn;
   (b) it has the greatest mileage of stone walls;
   (c) it has one of the highest sheets of permanent standing water, and,
       in springtime, the highest resident population of tadpoles;
   (d) it has the purest mountain form;
   (e) it has the reddest screes and the greenest stone;
   (f) it has one of the finest views (but not the most extensive nor the
       most beautiful) and <u>the</u> finest of the High Street range;
   (g) it has the easiest way down;
   (h) it offers alcoholic beverages at 1480';
   (i) it gives birth to the stream with the most beautiful waterfalls.
      {Some of these statements are expressions of opinion;
               others, especially (h), are hard facts}

Saint Sunday Crag 2756'

Glenridding

Patterdale

▲ HELVELLYN

ST SUNDAY
CRAG ▲

Hartsop

▲ FAIRFIELD

MILES

0   1   2   3   4

from Ullswater

NATURAL FEATURES

The slender soaring lines of St Sunday Crag and its aloof height and steepness endow this fine mountain with special distinction. It stands on a triangular base and its sides rise with such regularity that all its contours assume the same shape, as does the final summit-plateau. Ridges ascend from the corners of the triangle to the top of the fell, the one best-defined naturally rising from the sharpest angle: this is the south-west ridge connecting with Fairfield at Deepdale Hause. A shorter rougher ridge runs down northeast to Birks. Due east of the top is a subsidiary peak, Gavel Pike, from which a broadening ridge falls to Deepdale. A fringe of crags, nearly a mile in length, overtops the Grisedale face, which drops nearly 2000 feet in height in a lateral distance of half-a-mile: in Lakeland, only Great Gable can show greater concentrated steepness over a similar fall in altitude. The south-east face is also steep but less impressive, and the easy slopes to the north-east break into foothills before dropping abruptly to valley-level in Patterdale: these slopes are the gathering grounds of Coldcove Gill, the main stream.

Every walker who aspires to high places and looks up at the remote summit of St Sunday Crag will experience an urge to go forth and climb up to it, for its challenge is very strong. Its rewards are equally generous, and altogether this is a noble fell. Saint Sunday must surely look down on his memorial with profound gratification.

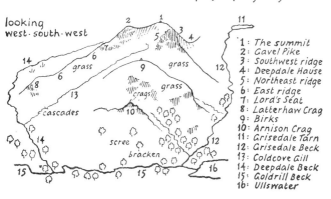

looking
west-south-west

1 : The summit
2 : Gavel Pike
3 : Southwest ridge
4 : Deepdale Hause
5 : Northeast ridge
6 : East ridge
7 : Lord's Seat
8 : Latterhaw Crag
9 : Birks
10 : Arnison Crag
11 : Grisedale Tarn
12 : Grisedale Beck
13 : Coldcove Gill
14 : Deepdale Beck
15 : Goldrill Beck
16 : Ullswater

NATURAL FEATURES

St Sunday Crag has an imposing appearance from whatever direction it is seen, an attribute rare in mountains. From Ullswater and from Grisedale its outline is very familiar; less well known (because less often seen) is its fine eastern aspect.

The East Ridge, from Dubhow

There is a glimpse, often unnoticed, of the lofty east ridge soaring high above Deepdale, from the roadway near Bridgend. A much better view is obtained from Dubhow, nearby on the old cart-track across the valley.

Cascades, Coldcove Gill

Summit of Gavel Pike

MAP

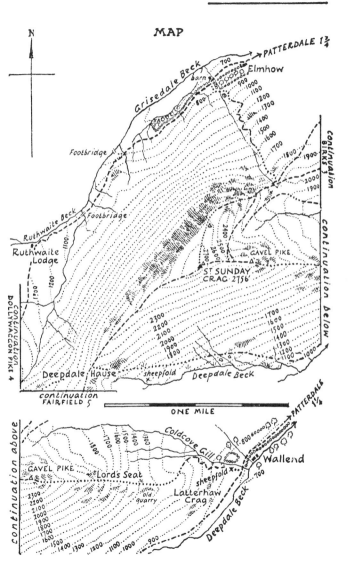

ASCENT FROM PATTERDALE
2300 feet of ascent : 3 miles (4 by East Ridge)

looking south-west

ST SUNDAY CRAG

GAVEL PIKE

East Ridge

DEEPDALE HAUSE

2700
2600
2500
2400
2300
2200
2100
2000
1900

Lord's Seat

1800

1700

1600

Latterhaw Crag

Coldove Gill

ruin x1

BIRKS

grass

grass

bracken

Black Crag

Trough Head

1300

stile

Hag Beck

1200

The Elmhow zig zag, once the popular route, has now fallen from favour. It is useful only for descent in mist

GRISEDALE TARN

scree
bracken

barn

Thornhow End

Elmhow

Grisedale Beck

bracken

sheepfold

900

800

Glemara Park

Wallend

ARNISON CRAG

1100

scree

bracken

gate

Further details of Arnison Crag and Birks will be found in the separate chapters on those fells.

900

800

Mill Moss

Church

Deepdale Beck

Deepdale Hall

gate

Patterdale

KIRKSTONE ←

Bridgend

The *easiest* route (not depicted) follows Deepdale to its head at Deepdale Hause, then ascends the southwest ridge. Apart from a short sharp pull on to the Hause there is no steep climbing. There are intimate views of the crags of Fairfield

The popular route is *via* Thornhow End and the western flank of Birks (in clear weather it is better to proceed over the top of Birks). The Trough Head route is easier but dull. The east ridge is an interesting alternative and technically the best line of ascent.

ASCENT FROM GRISEDALE TARN
1000 feet of ascent · 1¼ miles

looking north·east

ST SUNDAY CRAG

The traverse from the tarn to Deepdale Hause is rough: there is no path, but there is need of one, and some public·spirited hiker with nothing better to do would serve his fellows well by stamping out a track and cairning it.

St Sunday Crag is commonly and correctly regarded as the preserve of Patterdale, yet it is interesting to note that the summit is less than three miles from the Keswick–Ambleside road at Dunmail Raise: it may be ascended easily and quickly from here. And from Grasmere *via* Tongue Gill.   In either case, the first objective is Grisedale Tarn.

St Sunday Crag
from Grisedale Tarn

THE SUMMIT

The summit hardly lives up to the promise of the ridges: it is merely a slight stony mound set on the edge of a plateau —a pleasant place of mosses and lichens and grey rocks, but quite unexciting. Two cairns adorn the top, and there is also a well-built column of stones a quarter of a mile away across the plateau to the north.

Gavel Pike has a much more attractive summit than the main fell: here are bilberries and heather and natural armchairs among the rocks of the tiny peaked top, and splendid views to enjoy. A delectable place for (packed) lunch!

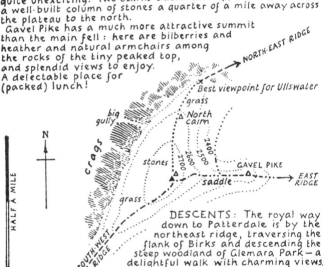

DESCENTS: The royal way down to Patterdale is by the northeast ridge, traversing the flank of Birks and descending the steep woodland of Glemara Park—a delightful walk with charming views. Other routes are very inferior. For Grisedale Tarn, use the southwest ridge to Deepdale Hause, thence slanting over rough ground to the tarn, which is in view.

In bad conditions, the danger lies in the long line of crags on the Grisedale face, this fortunately being preceded by steep ground which serves as a warning. For Patterdale, the path from the saddle is safest. To find Deepdale Hause in mist, leave the top with the two cairns in line behind.

Ullswater
from the
north-east ridge

RIDGE ROUTES

To FAIRFIELD, 2863' : 1½ miles : SW then S
Depression at 2150' : 750 feet of ascent
A simple descent followed by rough scrambling

A very pleasant stroll down the south-west ridge, on grass, leads to the depression of Deepdale Hause. From here, Cofa Pike looks quite formidable, but a plain path climbs steeply up the stony slope to the interesting crest of the Pike. A loose scree slope is then climbed to the grassy shoulder above and the summit-cairn is just beyond. *In mist, Fairfield is a dangerous place to strangers.*

ST SUNDAY CRAG

2600
2500
2400
2700
2200
2100

N

HALF A MILE

Deepdale Hause
DEEPDALE
GRISEDALE TARN

Cofa Pike
2200
2300
2400
2500
2700
FAIRFIELD

To BIRKS, 2040' : 1¼ miles : NE
Minor depressions : 50 feet of ascent

An easy walk with delightful views
Cross the tilted summit-plateau to the north cairn; beyond, the north-east ridge goes down to a col, whence a level grassy path leads on to Birks.

ELMHOW
THORNHOW END
BIRKS
2000
Col
1900
TROUGH HEAD

2000
2100
2200
2300
2400
2500
2600
Gavel Pike
ST SUNDAY CRAG

The view from the north cairn

GREAT MELL FELL
LITTLE MELL FELL
COWBARROW FELL
BIRK FELL
PLACE FELL
GLENRIDDING DODD
BIRKHOUSE MOOR
BIRKS

THE VIEW

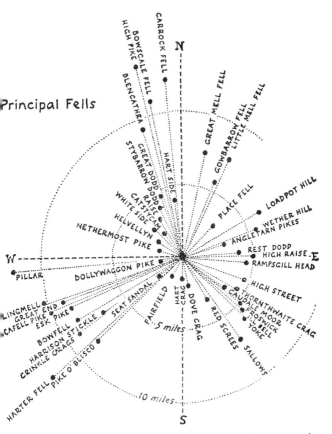

Principal Fells

The walker who reaches the summit eagerly expecting to see the classic view of Ullswater from St Sunday Crag will be disappointed —he must go to the bristly rocks at the top of the north-east ridge for that. The lake makes a beautiful picture also from the saddle leading to Gavel Pike. Helvellyn is a fine study in mountain structure, and the best aspect of Fairfield is seen, but these two fells restrict the view. The High Street range, however, is well seen.

Lakes and Tarns
NE : *Ullswater*
E : *Angle Tarn*

Seat Sandal

2415'

from Grasmere

HELVELLYN
▲

FAIRFIELD
▲
SEAT SANDAL ▲

Grasmere
●

MILES
0   1   2

Cascade, Raise Beck

NATURAL FEATURES

Prominent in the Grasmere landscape is the lofty outline of Seat Sandal, soaring gracefully from Dunmail Raise to the flat-topped summit and then suddenly falling away in a steep plunge eastwards. This view reveals its character well: the western flanks are smooth curves of grass and bracken, but the eastern face is a rough slope of shattered cliff and tumbled rock and loose scree from which rises abruptly an overhanging crag. Seat Sandal is a simple straightforward fell, uninteresting except as a viewpoint, with no dramatic effects, no hidden surprises. Geographically it belongs to Fairfield, to which it is connected by a low ridge crossed by the Grisedale Pass.

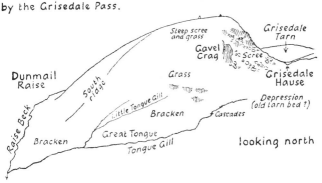

looking north

Seat Sandal has one distinction: its waters reach the sea at more widely divergent points than those of any other Lakeland fell. This has been so since the diversion of Raise Beck to feed Thirlmere. (*Dollywaggon Pike shares this distinction only when Raise Beck is flowing south at Dunmail Raise*)

1 : Raise Beck —
  to Thirlmere and (that which escapes being sent back south over Dunmail to Manchester) via Derwentwater to the sea at Workington.

2 : Raise Beck and Tongue Gill —
  to Grasmere, Windermere and Morecambe Bay.

3 : Grisedale Beck —
  to Ullswater and the Solway Firth.

MAP

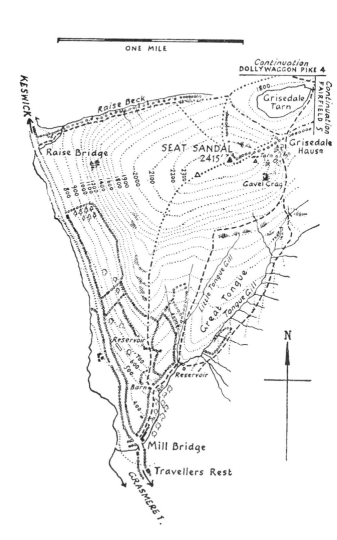

ASCENT FROM GRASMERE
2200 feet of ascent: 3½ miles from Grasmere Church

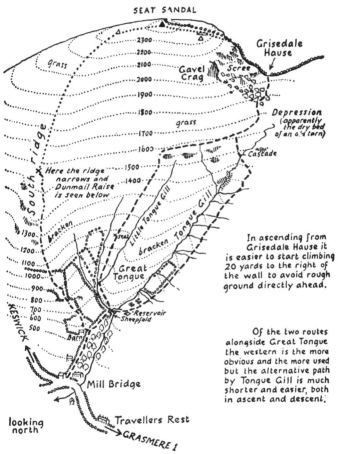

SEAT SANDAL

Grisedale Hause

Gavel Crag

Scree

grass

2300
2200
2100
2000
1900
1800
1700
1600
1500
1400

Depression
(apparently
the dry bed
of an old tarn)

grass

Cascade

South ridge

Here the ridge
narrows and
Dunmail Raise
is seen below

bracken

Little Tongue Gill

Tongue Gill

bracken

1300
1200
1100
1000
900
800
700
600
500

Great
Tongue

In ascending from
Grisedale Hause it
is easier to start climbing
20 yards to the right of
the wall to avoid rough
ground directly ahead.

Reservoir
Sheepfold

Barn

Of the two routes
alongside Great Tongue
the western is the more
obvious and the more used
but the alternative path
by Tongue Gill is much
shorter and easier, both
in ascent and descent.

KESWICK

Mill Bridge

looking
north

Travellers Rest

GRASMERE 1

The path to Grisedale Hause, by either side of the Tongue,
is distinct, but there is no track above the Hause or on the
upper part of the south ridge. If returning to Grasmere, it
is better to ascend by the Hause and descend by the ridge.

ASCENT FROM DUNMAIL RAISE
1700 feet of ascent : 1½ miles

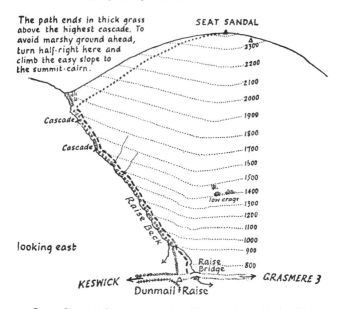

The path ends in thick grass above the highest cascade. To avoid marshy ground ahead, turn half-right here and climb the easy slope to the summit-cairn.

SEAT SANDAL

2300
2200
2100
2000
1900
1800
1700
1600
1500
1400
low crags
1300
1200
1100
1000
900
800

Cascade

Cascade

Raise Beck

looking east

Raise Bridge

KESWICK ← → GRASMERE 3

Dunmail Raise

Seat Sandal is very easily climbed from Raise Bridge. The direct route by the shoulder is not recommended: it is preferable to commence the ascent by using the rough path alongside the beck. This is a quick way up.

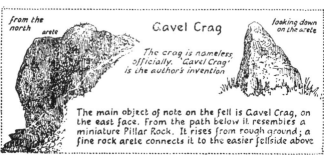

from the north arete

Gavel Crag

looking down on the arete

The crag is nameless officially. 'Gavel Crag' is the author's invention

The main object of note on the fell is Gavel Crag, on the east face. From the path below it resembles a miniature Pillar Rock. It rises from rough ground; a fine rock arete connects it to the easier fellside above

THE SUMMIT

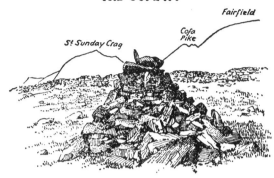

The summit is a flat grassy plateau with small stony outcrops. A broken wall crosses the top. The main cairn stands 30 yards west of the wall; two other cairns indicate alternative viewpoints.

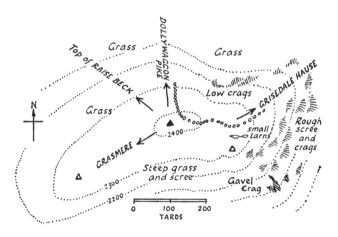

DESCENTS : The best way off the summit, in clear weather, is by the south ridge to Grasmere, the views being excellent and the gradient exactly right — this is one of the quickest descents in the district. All routes are safe in good conditions. There are no paths on the summit. The east face is steep, and should be avoided. In bad weather conditions, the safest descent is to Grisedale Hause (by the wall) where good paths lead to Grasmere and Patterdale.

THE VIEW

Principal Fells

Most of the interest in the view is in the western arc, where the panorama is excellent. In other directions, nearby Helvellyn and Fairfield limit the distant view. Many lakes and tarns are visible.

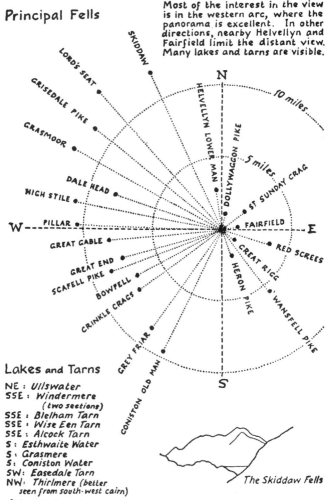

Lakes and Tarns

NE : *Ullswater*
SSE : *Windermere*
    (two sections)
SSE : *Blelham Tarn*
SSE : *Wise Een Tarn*
SSE : *Alcock Tarn*
S : *Eshthwaite Water*
S : *Grasmere*
S : *Coniston Water*
SW : *Easedale Tarn*
NW : *Thirlmere* (better
   seen from south-west cairn)

The Skiddaw Fells

Grisedale Tarn is seen by walking NE 150 yards from the summit-cairn.

RIDGE ROUTES

To FAIRFIELD, 2863': 1⅓ miles: E then NE and E.
Depression at 1929': 950 feet of ascent

A rough descent followed by a steep continuous climb. The top of Fairfield is confusing and dangerous in mist to anyone who is not familiar with it, but there is no difficulty in clear weather.

The wall is a guide down to Grisedale Hause: the last part of the descent is rough but there is easier ground just to the left. The wall continues up the shoulder of Fairfield to 2400' and gives up the struggle but the determined walker toils on along a fair path. The final part of the climb, much easier but without a path, follows a line of cairns across grass to the stony top.

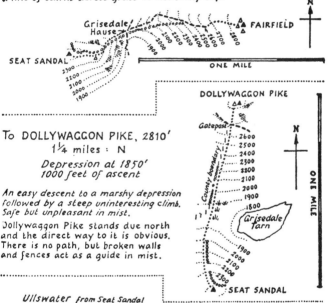

To DOLLYWAGGON PIKE, 2810'
1¼ miles: N
Depression at 1850'
1000 feet of ascent

An easy descent to a marshy depression followed by a steep uninteresting climb. Safe but unpleasant in mist.

Dollywaggon Pike stands due north and the direct way to it is obvious. There is no path, but broken walls and fences act as a guide in mist.

Ullswater from Seat Sandal

Sheffield Pike

2232'

from Glenridding

GREAT DODD
▲

Glencoyne
●

SHEFFIELD PIKE ▲

Glenridding
●

Patterdale
◎

HELVELLYN
▲

MILES

0 1 2 3 4 5

NATURAL FEATURES

Stybarrow Dodd, on the main Helvellyn watershed, has a long eastern shoulder falling in stages to the shore of Ullswater. Midway, the shoulder rises to a distinct and isolated summit: this is Sheffield Pike, which assumes the characteristics of a separate fell. It soars abruptly between the valleys of Glenridding and Glencoyne and it presents to each a continuous fringe of steep crags. The eastern aspect is pleasing, with rock and heather and an occasional rowan mingling above well-wooded slopes, but westwards the fell is drab and, in the environs of a vast lead mine, hideously scarred and downright ugly. Its rich mineral deposits have, paradoxically, caused its ruin: it has been robbed not only of its lead but of its appeal and attractiveness to walkers.

looking north-west

Heron Pike, from the east

MAP

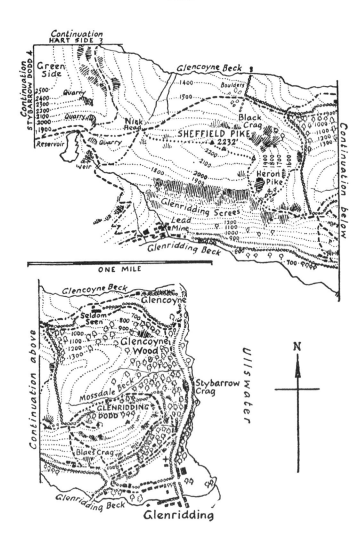

ASCENT FROM GLENRIDDING
1800 feet of ascent: 2 (or 3¼) miles

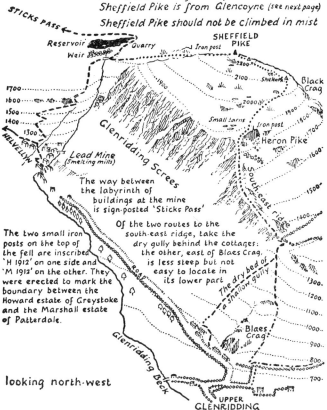

The evidences of industrialism are rampant in mid-Glenridding. The pleasantest way up Sheffield Pike is from Glencoyne (see next page)

Sheffield Pike should not be climbed in mist

STICKS PASS ←

Reservoir
Weir
Quarry
Iron post
SHEFFIELD PIKE
2200
Shelter
Black Crag
2100
2000
Small tarns
Iron post
1900
1800
1700
1600
Heron Pike
1700
1600
1500
1400
1300
HELVELLYN
Lead Mine (Smelting mills)
1900
1800
Glenridding Screes
South-east ridge
1500
1400
1300
1200
1100
1000
900
800
700

The way between the labyrinth of buildings at the mine is sign-posted 'Sticks Pass'

Of the two routes to the south-east ridge, take the dry gully behind the cottages: the other, east of Blaes Crag, is less steep but not easy to locate in its lower part

The two small iron posts on the top of the fell are inscribed 'H 1912' on one side and 'M 1912' on the other. They were erected to mark the boundary between the Howard estate of Greystoke and the Marshall estate of Patterdale.

The dry bed of a shallow gully

Road
Glenridding Beck
Blaes Crag

looking north-west

UPPER GLENRIDDING

Of the two routes illustrated, the climb up the ridge is much to be preferred, but it is steep and rough. The path zig-zagging above the smelting mills is longer and easier —but much less inspiring and not at all exhilarating.

ASCENT FROM GLENCOYNE
1800 feet of ascent : 2½ miles

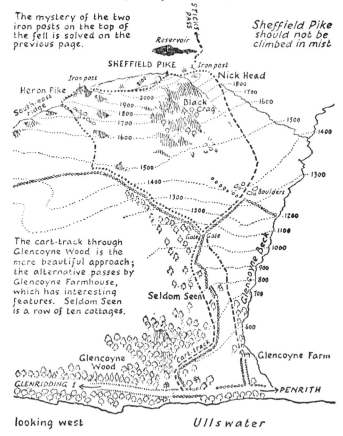

The mystery of the two iron posts on the top of the fell is solved on the previous page.

Sheffield Pike should not be climbed in mist

STICKS PASS

Reservoir

SHEFFIELD PIKE

Iron post

Nick Head

Iron post

Heron Pike

South-east ridge

Black Crag

Boulders

Gate Gate

Glencoyne Beck

The cart-track through Glencoyne Wood is the more beautiful approach; the alternative passes by Glencoyne Farmhouse, which has interesting features. Seldom Seen is a row of ten cottages.

Seldom Seen

Glencoyne Wood

cart-track

Glencoyne Farm

GLENRIDDING 1

PENRITH

looking west

Ullswater

It is usual to follow the path to Nick Head and there turn east to the summit: this is the easiest of all ways on to the fell. Far more attractive, however, is a route traversing below Heron Pike to the top of the south-east ridge, the walking being easy and the views excellent: this is one of the pleasantest short climbs in Lakeland.

THE SUMMIT

Even on a sunny summer day the top of the fell seems a dismal, cheerless place; the vicinity of the cairn above Black Crag, and the top of Heron Pike, where there is heather, are both nicer.
There are many slight undulations and craggy outcrops. Marshy ground occurs in several places and there are many small tarns.

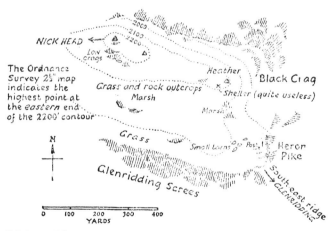

The Ordnance Survey 2½" map indicates the highest point at the *eastern* end of the 2200' contour

NICK HEAD

Low crags

2000
2100
2200

Heather

Black Crag

Grass and rock outcrops
Marsh

Shelter (quite useless)

Marsh

N

Grass

Small tarns

Post

Heron Pike

Glenridding Screes

south-east ridge
GLENRIDDING

0   100   200   300   400
YARDS

DESCENTS: Any of the routes of ascent may be reversed in clear weather, the south-east ridge being incomparably the best. Some care is necessary in getting off Heron Pike on to the ridge. There are no paths on the summit, which has crags on all sides except westwards. In bad weather conditions, the only safe way is due west to Nick Head (very gradual descent, boggy in places), from there preferably following the good path down to Glencoyne.

THE VIEW

Ullswater is the main feature of a restricted view. Westwards the prospect is dull; it is really good only between north-east and south. Heron Pike is a much finer viewpoint.

Principal Fells

N

5 miles

2½ miles

GREAT MELL FELL

LITTLE MELL FELL

GOWBARROW FELL

GREAT DODD

HART SIDE

STYBARROW DODD

W — — — — — — — — E

LOADPOT HILL

RAISE

PLACE FELL

WETHER HILL

WHITE SIDE

LOWER MAN

CATSTYCAM

HELVELLYN

HELVELLYN

BIRKHOUSE MOOR

FAIRFIELD

ST. SUNDAY CRAG

RED SCREES

CAUDALE MOOR

THORNTHWAITE CRAG

HIGH STREET

RAMPSGILL HEAD

HIGH RAISE

S

Lakes and Tarns

NE : Ullswater (better seen from the cairn above Black Crag and from Heron Pike)

SE : Lanty's Tarn

W : Reservoir, below Sticks Pass

Black Crag

Heron Pike

RIDGE ROUTES

To STYBARROW DODD, 2770' : 2 miles : W then NW and W.
Depression at 1925' : 1000 feet of ascent

A simple walk with a long climb on grass midway. No path.

An easy descent westwards, boggy in places, leads to Nick Head. Cross the indistinct paths here and climb the long grassy slope ahead to the cairn on Green Side. Stybarrow Dodd is then in view in front, across a shallow depression. *This route is not recommended in bad conditions.*

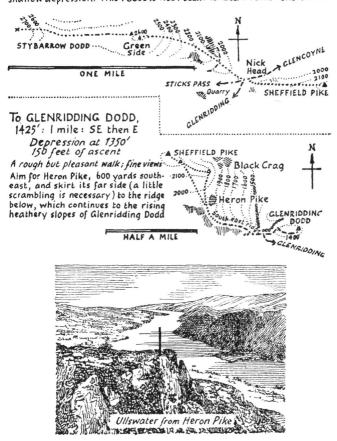

STYBARROW DODD   Green Side

ONE MILE

Nick Head   GLENCOYNE

STICKS PASS

Quarry

GLENRIDDING

SHEFFIELD PIKE

To GLENRIDDING DODD, 1425' : 1 mile : SE then E
Depression at 1350' 150 feet of ascent

A rough but pleasant walk; fine views

Aim for Heron Pike, 600 yards south-east, and skirt its far side (a little scrambling is necessary) to the ridge below, which continues to the rising heathery slopes of Glenridding Dodd

SHEFFIELD PIKE

Black Crag

Heron Pike

GLENRIDDING DODD

South-east ridge

GLENRIDDING

HALF A MILE

Ullswater from Heron Pike

Stone Arthur

sometimes referred to as Arthur's Chair

from Grasmere

▲ FAIRFIELD

▲ GREAT RIGG

▲ STONE ARTHUR

▲ HERON PIKE

Grasmere ○ ▲ NAB SCAR

● Rydal

Ambleside ○

MILES
0   1   2   3   4

Without its prominent tor of steep rock, Stone Arthur would probably never have been given a name for it is merely the abrupt end of a spur of Great Rigg although it has the appearance of a separate fell when seen from Grasmere. The outcrop occurs where the gradual decline of the spur becomes pronounced and here are the short walls of rock, like a ruined castle, that give Stone Arthur its one touch of distinction.

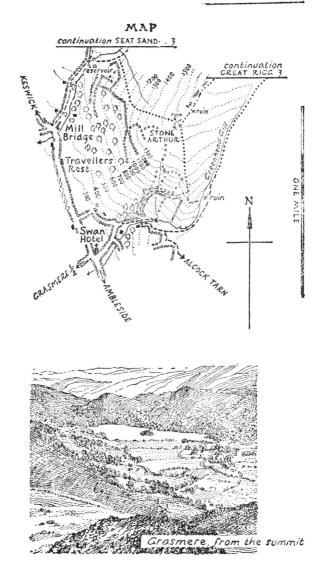

MAP

continuation SEAT SAND. 3

continuation GREAT RIGG 3

KESWICK

reservoir

1200 1300 1400 1700

ruin x ruin

Mill Bridge

STONE ARTHUR

Travellers Rest

500 600 700 800

Greenhead Gill

x ruin

N

Swan Hotel

ALCOCK TARN

GRASMERE ½

AMBLESIDE

ONE MILE

Grasmere, from the summit

THE VIEW

The gem of the view is Easedale Tarn in its wild setting among colourful fells with a towering background culminating in Scafell Pike. The vale of Grasmere, below, is also attractive. The southern ridge of Fairfield occupies the whole horizon to the east, uninterestingly.

Principal Fells

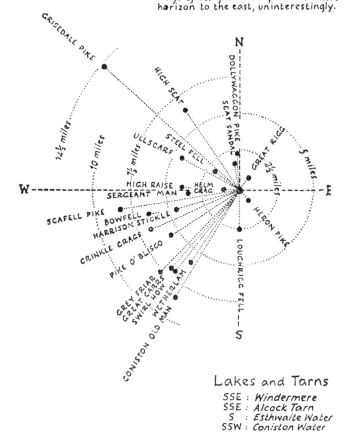

Lakes and Tarns

SSE : *Windermere*
SSE : *Alcock Tarn*
S : *Esthwaite Water*
SSW : *Coniston Water*
SSW : *Grasmere*
WSW : *Easedale Tarn*

ASCENT FROM GRASMERE

Use the lane alongside the Swan Hotel : the second turning on the right leads to a track alongside Greenhead Gill. At the gate turn left : an overgrown path winds round the steep slope ahead between walls. When the open fell is reached incline left to the prominent rocky summit.

THE SUMMIT

from the west

The break in the continuity of the fall along the shoulder is so slight that it is not easy to define the summit exactly; there is no cairn. The height 1652', a survey triangulation point, may well be a big embedded boulder on the highest part of the rocky extremity. The small crags around the summit offer practice for embryo climbers whose main concern is not to drop too far if they fall.

DESCENTS : To find the Grasmere path, aim directly for Alcock Tarn. In mist, any way down is safe after the initial crags are left behind, but unless the path can be found the thick bracken will prove an abomination.

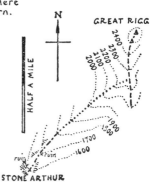

RIDGE ROUTE

To GREAT RIGG, 2513'
1¼ miles : NE then N
Easy climbing all the way
Follow the shoulder upwards; when it widens and becomes altogether grassy incline right to the ridge. Safe in mist.

Stybarrow Dodd

2770'
approx.

from Brown Crag

Dockray

▲ GREAT DODD

STYBARROW
▲ DODD

Stanah
Thirlspot

Glencoyne

▲ RAISE

Glenridding

▲ HELVELLYN

MILES

0   1   2   3   4

NATURAL FEATURES

Stybarrow Dodd is the first of the group of fells north of the Sticks Pass and it sets the pattern for them all: sweeping grassy slopes, easy walking for the traveller who likes to count his miles but rather wearisome for those who prefer to see rock in the landscape. Rock is so rare that the slightest roughnesses get undeserved identification on most maps, either by distinctive name or extravagant hachures: thus Deepdale Crag is hardly more than a short stony slope. Stybarrow Dodd sends out a long eastern spur that rises to a minor height, Green Side (which, incidentally, gives its name to the lead mine in nearby Glenridding) before falling steeply to Glencoyne; on Green Side there are both crags and dangerous quarries, now disused.

Stybarrow Dodd's one proud distinction is that on its slopes it carries the well-known path over Sticks Pass throughout most of its length. Far more people ascend the slopes of Stybarrow Dodd than reach its summit!

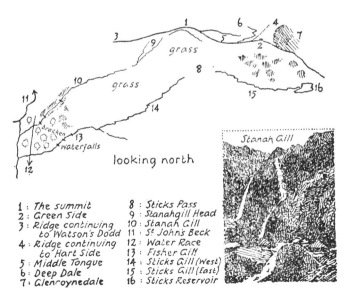

looking north

Stanah Gill

1 : The summit
2 : Green Side
3 : Ridge continuing to Watson's Dodd
4 : Ridge continuing to Hart Side
5 : Middle Tongue
6 : Deep Dale
7 : Glenroynedale
8 : Sticks Pass
9 : Stanahgill Head
10 : Stanah Gill
11 : St John's Beck
12 : Water Race
13 : Fisher Gill
14 : Sticks Gill (West)
15 : Sticks Gill (East)
16 : Sticks Reservoir

MAP

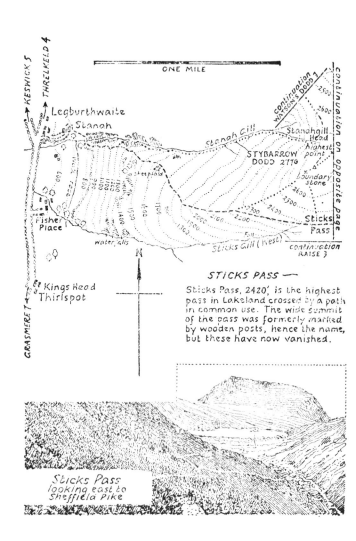

ONE MILE

KESWICK 5
THRELKELD 4
GRASMERE 1
RAISE 3

Legburthwaite
Stanah
Stanah Gill
Stanahgill Head
highest point
STYBARROW DODD 2770
boundary stone
Sticks Pass
Sticks Gill (West)
continuation RAISE 3
continuation WATSON'S DODD 3
continuation on opposite page
sheepfold
waterfalls
Fisher Place
Kings Head Thirlspot

2500
2600
2700
2600
2500
1000
900
800
700
1000
1100
1200
1300
1400
1500
1600
1700
1800
1900
2000

N

STICKS PASS —

Sticks Pass, 2420', is the highest pass in Lakeland crossed by a path in common use. The wide summit was formerly marked by wooden posts, hence the name, but these have now vanished.

Sticks Pass
looking east to
Sheffield Pike

MAP

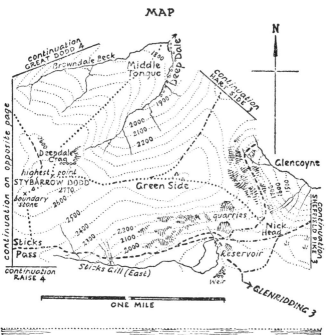

continuation GREAT DODD 4

Browndale Beck

Middle Tongue

1800

Deep Dale

continuation HART SIDE

N

continuation on opposite page

Deepdale Crag

highest point
STYBARROW DODD

boundary stone

2770

1900

2000

2100

2200

Green Side

Glencoyne

continuation SHEFFIELD PIKE 3

2600

2500

2400

2300

2200

2100

2000

quarries

Nick Head

1500

1600

1700

Sticks Pass

Sticks Gill (East)

Weir

reservoir

GLENRIDDING 3

continuation RAISE 4

ONE MILE

Ullswater
from the east slope of
Green Side

ASCENT FROM STANAH
2300 feet of ascent : 2½ miles

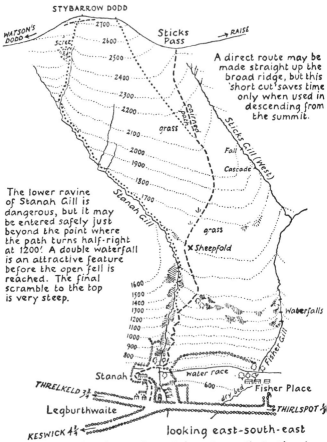

WATSON'S DODD ←

STYBARROW DODD

2700

2600

Scree

2500

2400

2300

2200

2100

grass

2000

1900

1800

1700

Sticks Pass

→ RAISE

A direct route may be made straight up the broad ridge, but this 'short cut' saves time only when used in descending from the summit.

cairned path

Sticks Gill (West)

Fall

Cascade

The lower ravine of Stanah Gill is dangerous, but it may be entered safely just beyond the point where the path turns half-right at 1200'. A double waterfall is an attractive feature before the open fell is reached. The final scramble to the top is very steep.

Stanah Gill

grass

✕ Sheepfold

1600
1500
1400
1300
1200
1100
1000
900
800

Waterfalls

Fisher Gill

Stanah

water race

600

dry bed

Fisher Place

THRELKELD 3¾

Legburthwaite

KESWICK 4¼

THIRLSPOT ½

looking east-south-east

Conveniently, the path to Sticks Pass climbs the slope of Stybarrow Dodd, the summit being easily gained from the top of the pass. Stanah Gill is a rough alternative affording some relief from the dull grassiness of the path

ASCENT FROM DOCKRAY
1900 feet of ascent : 5½ miles

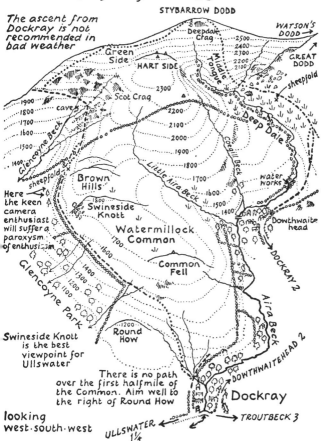

STYBARROW DODD

The ascent from Dockray is not recommended in bad weather

WATSON'S DODD

Deepdale Crag

Green Side

HART SIDE

Middle Tongue

GREAT DODD

sheepfold

2500
2400
2300
2200
2100

2300

Scot Crag

Deep Dale

1900
1800
1700
1600
1500
1400

cave

Glencoyne Beck

2200
2100
2000
1900
1800

Coegill Beck

sheepfold

Brown Hills

Little Aira Beck

1700

1600

1500

1400

water works

Here the keen camera enthusiast will suffer a paroxysm of enthusiasm

Swineside Knott

Watermillock Common

1800

Dowthwaite head

Glencoyne Park

1600

1700

Common Fell

DOCKRAY 2

1400

1200

1100

Aira Beck

Round How

1200

Swineside Knott is the best viewpoint for Ullswater

DOWTHWAITEHEAD 2

There is no path over the first half mile of the Common. Aim well to the right of Round How

Dockray

looking west·south·west

ULLSWATER 1¼

TROUTBECK 3

There is all the difference in the world between the two routes depicted. The direct way by Deep Dale is dreary and depressing ; that by the Brown Hills is (after a dull start) a splendid high-level route, excelling in its views of Ullswater below.

THE SUMMIT

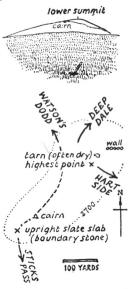

lower summit

cairn

The summit, all grass, is quite devoid of interest, and the walker may care to spend his few minutes' rest by first determining the highest point of the Dodd and then estimating its altitude.

The usually-accepted top is the upright slate slab at the south-western end, (2756'), but there is higher ground 300 yards north-east, indicated by a very loose (at the time of writing!) estate-boundary iron post That it *is* higher is easily proved : from here, the slate slab at 2756' is seen to cover a part of Esk Pike, 9½ miles away, at about 2400'; therefore the view is *downward*. Q.E.D.

The altitude of the highest point can be roughly decided mathematically. It will be noted that the summit of Raise (2889', 7 furlongs) is directly below the summit of Helvellyn (3080' say, 18 furlongs). The walker didn't climb up here to do sums, and is not likely to challenge the statement that the altitude may, from the data, be calculated at 2770' approximately.

The Ordnance Survey maps are so wonderfully accurate that it needs confidence to suggest that an error has been made in the contouring of the 2½" map, which wrongly shows contours rising to 2825'. The 1"map is correct.

DESCENTS : All ways off are obvious in clear weather. Think twice before dropping down into Deep Dale. *In bad conditions aim south for Sticks Pass.*

RIDGE ROUTE

To RAISE, 2889' : 1 mile : SW then S
Depression at 2420'(Sticks Pass)
470 feet of ascent

An easy walk, mostly on grass. Safe in mist.
From the boundary stone, descend south to cross Sticks Pass at its highest point. The long facing slope of Raise becomes stony towards the summit

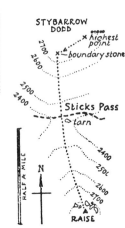

RIDGE ROUTES

To WATSON'S DODD, 2584': ⅔ mile : NW
Depression slight · Ascent negligible

A very easy stroll. Safe in mist.
A boundary stone and a small tarn
are the only features. A faint path
crosses the depression but does not
lead to the summit cairn, which is
easily reached by inclining left,
slightly ascending across the flat
plateau. Beware marshy ground.

- -

To HART SIDE, 2481': 1½ miles : E then NE
Depressions at 2525' and 2250': 300 feet of ascent

An easy walk on grass. Not recommended in mist.
Descend east, leaving the wall well to the left,
to the obvious ridge rising gently to Green Side.
Skirt the cairns there and aim directly for
Hart Side ahead. Crags and quarries on the
flanks of Green Side make this route
unsafe in bad weather conditions.

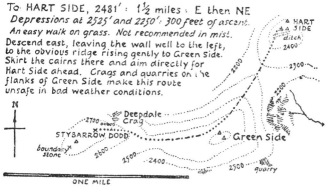

To SHEFFIELD PIKE, 2232': 2 miles : E then SE and E
Depressions at 2525' and 1925': 400 feet of ascent
An easy walk. Not recommended in mist.

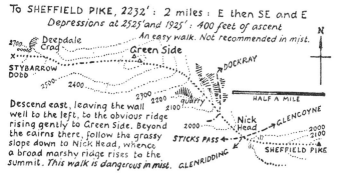

Descend east, leaving the wall
well to the left, to the obvious ridge
rising gently to Green Side. Beyond
the cairns there, follow the grassy
slope down to Nick Head, whence
a broad marshy ridge rises to the
summit. *This walk is dangerous in mist.*

THE VIEW

An extensive and excellent panorama
is seen above a dull and dreary foreground

Principal Fells

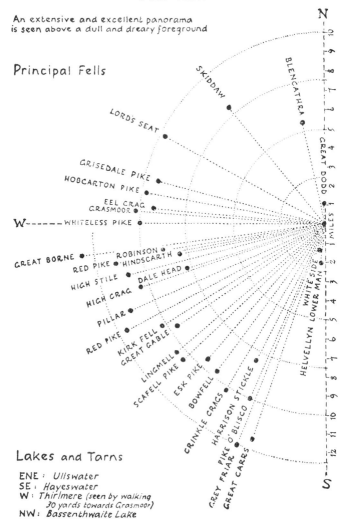

Lakes and Tarns

ENE : *Ullswater*
SE : *Hayeswater*
W : *Thirlmere (seen by walking*
30 yards towards Grasmoor)
NW : *Bassenthwaite Lake*

THE VIEW

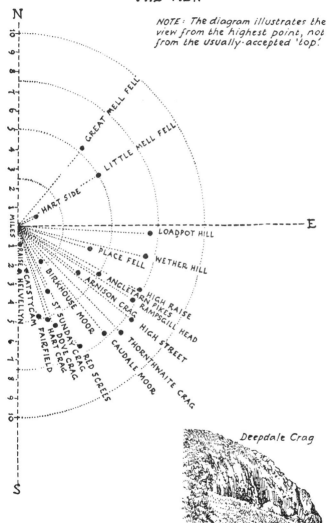

NOTE: The diagram illustrates the view from the highest point, not from the usually·accepted 'top'.

N

10
9
8
7
6
5
4
3
2
1

1 MILES

E

2
3
4
5
6
7
8
9
10

S

GREAT MELL FELL

LITTLE MELL FELL

HART SIDE

LOADPOT HILL

PLACE FELL

WETHER HILL

HIGH RAISE

ANGLETARN PIKES

RAMPSGILL HEAD

ARNISON CRAG

HIGH STREET

THORNTHWAITE CRAG

CAUDALE MOOR

RAISE

HELVELLYN

CATSTYCAM

BIRKHOUSE MOOR

ST SUNDAY CRAG

DOVE CRAG

HART CRAG

FAIRFIELD

RED SCREES

Deepdale Crag

Watson's Dodd 2584'

▲ GREAT DODD
▲ WATSON'S DODD
● Legburthwaite
● Thirlspot

▲ HELVELLYN

MILES
0 1 2 3 4

from Smaithwaite

NATURAL FEATURES

Whoever Mr. Watson may have been, it is a very odd Dodd that has been selected to perpetuate his name. A separate fell it is undoubtedly, with boundaries unusually sharply defined on north and south by deep ravines, but although it conforms to normal mountain structure on three sides — west, north and south — it has no eastern flanks at all: the slope going down east to Deep Dale from the summit-plateau is bisected by a stream that clearly divides Great Dodd and Stybarrow Dodd, and Watson's Dodd cannot stake a claim to any land on this side. In other respects the fell is normal, taking the form of a steepsided ridge, mainly grass with a fringe of crag. With Great Dodd it shares ownership of a very fine ravine, the little-known Mill Gill, but its especial pride and joy is the Castle Rock of Triermain, an imposing and familiar object overlooking the Vale of St. John.

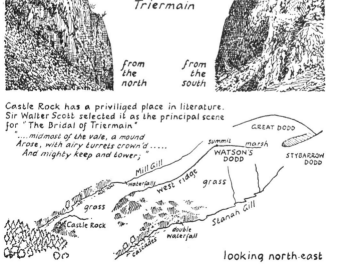

The
Castle Rock
of
Triermain

from
the
north

from
the
south

Castle Rock has a priviliged place in literature.
Sir Walter Scott selected it as the principal scene
for "The Bridal of Triermain"

"...midmost of the vale, a mound
Arose, with airy turrets crown'd.....
And mighty keep and tower;"

GREAT DODD

summit   marsh
WATSON'S
DODD   STYBARROW
                        DODD

Mill Gill

Waterfalls   west ridge   grass

grass

Castle Rock

double
waterfall

cascades

Stanah Gill

looking north-east

MAP

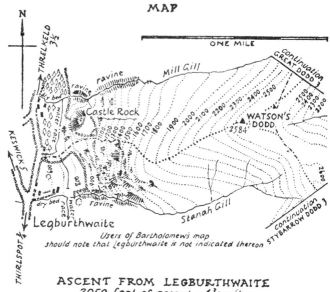

N

ONE MILE

THRELKELD 3½

KESWICK 5

THIRLSPOT 4

Mill Gill

ravine

ravine

dry bed

water race

Castle Rock

1100 1200 1300 1400 1500 1600 1700 1800 1900 2000 2100 2200 2300 2400 2500

continuation GREAT DODD 3

2500 2400 2300 2200

WATSON'S DODD 2584

OLD RACE

dry bed race

water race

ravine

Stanah Gill

2500 2400 2300 2200

continuation STYBARROW DODD 3

Legburthwaite

Users of Bartholomew's map should note that Legburthwaite is not indicated thereon

ASCENT FROM LEGBURTHWAITE
2050 feet of ascent : 1¾ miles

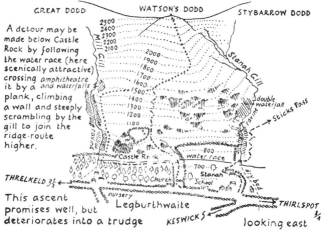

GREAT DODD

WATSON'S DODD

STYBARROW DODD

A detour may be made below Castle Rock by following the water race (here scenically attractive) crossing *amphitheatre and waterfalls* it by a plank, climbing a wall and steeply scrambling by the gill to join the ridge-route higher.

2500 2400 2300 2200 2100

2000 1900 1800 1700 1600 1500 1400 1300 1200 1100

Gill

amphitheatre and waterfalls

Stanah Gill

double waterfall

ravine

Sticks Pass

RAVINE

Castle Rock

800 water race

700

Stanah School

THRELKELD 3½

nursery

Church

Legburthwaite

KESWICK 5

THIRLSPOT ¾

This ascent promises well, but deteriorates into a trudge

looking east

THE SUMMIT

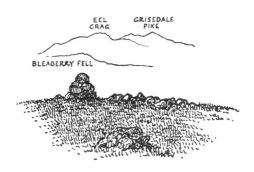

A few big stones adorn the highest point, at the western end of the flat triangular top, and they look strangely alien just there in the universal grassiness of the surroundings, as though they had been carried there. (Maybe Mr. Watson undertook this task: if so, it is fitting that the fell should bear his name!). There is a suggestion of history in these hoary stones.

DESCENTS : The quickest way down to civilisation is by the west ridge, which commences immediately below the cairn. After half a mile, when the ground becomes rough, incline right to avoid crags ahead and aim for the south corner of the wall behind Castle Rock ; an old path in a groove leads down to it and continues to the valley. *In mist*, use the same route : the ridge is fairly well defined, but if in doubt incline right rather than left. Avoid getting into Mill Gill or Stanah Gill, both of which are dangerous.

RIDGE ROUTES

To GREAT DODD, 2807' : ¾ mile : NE
Depression imperceptible: 250 feet of ascent
An easy walk on grass. Safe but confusing in mist.
There is a complete absence of landmarks.
No path connects the two tops, but several
cross the depression. Beware marshy ground.

To STYBARROW DODD, 2770' :
⅔ mile : SE .
Depression slight: 200 feet of ascent
An easy walk on grass. Safe in mist.
A boundary stone and a small tarn are
the only features. A faint path will be
found at the depression. There is no
cairn on the highest point, near a wall.

Castle Rock and Mill Gill

THE VIEW

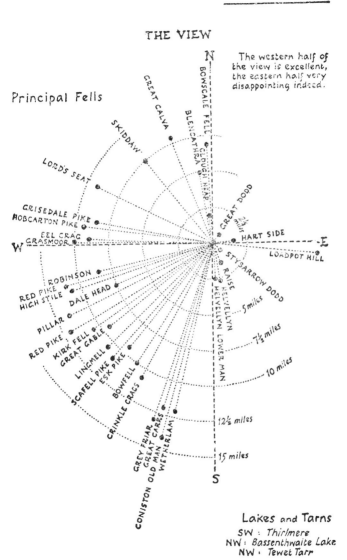

The western half of the view is excellent, the eastern half very disappointing indeed.

Principal Fells

N

GREAT CALVA
BOWSCALE FELL
CLOUGH HEAD
BLENCATHRA
SKIDDAW
GREAT DODD
LORD'S SEAT
HART SIDE
GRISEDALE PIKE
HOBCARTON PIKE
LOADPOT HILL
EEL CRAG
GRASMOOR
STYBARROW DODD
RAISE
ROBINSON
HELVELLYN
RED PIKE
HELVELLYN LOWER MAN
HIGH STILE
DALE HEAD
5 miles
PILLAR
7½ miles
RED PIKE
KIRK FELL
GREAT GABLE
10 miles
LINGMELL
SCAFELL PIKE
ESK PIKE
BOWFELL
12½ miles
CRINKLE CRAGS
15 miles
GREY FRIAR
GREAT CARRS
CONISTON OLD MAN
WETHERLAM

W — E

S

Lakes and Tarns
SW : Thirlmere
NW : Bassenthwaite Lake
NW : Tewet Tarn

White Side

— a name of convenience.
The summit is strictly nameless,
White Side being the west slope
below the top (probably so-called
from splashes of quartz on many
of the stones).

△ GREAT DODD

Thirlspot
●
RAISE ▲   Glenridding
                        ●
     ▲ WHITE SIDE
          ▲ CATSTYCAM
     ▲ HELVELLYN

● Wythburn
          MILES
  0   1   2   3   4

from Catstycam

NATURAL FEATURES

Although White Side presents an intimidating wall of low crags to travellers on the road at Thirlspot its upper slopes on this western side are docile enough, being wholly of grass at easy gradients: two paths to Helvellyn cross this flank. Very different is the eastern face, which falls sharply and steeply in crag and scree to the silent recesses of the wild upper Glenridding valley.

The summit is no more than a big grassy mound on the high ridge running northwards from Helvellyn and it rises only slightly above the general level of the ridge.

Skiers and sheep share a high regard for White Side.

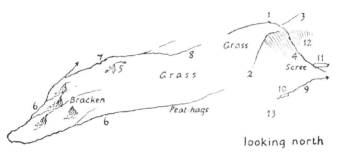

looking north

1: The summit
2: Ridge continuing to Helvellyn Lower Man
3: Ridge continuing to Raise
4: The east ridge
5: Brown Crag
6: Helvellyn Gill
7: Fisher Gill
8: Brund Gill
9: Glenridding Beck
10: Tarn in Brown Cove
11: Keppelcove Tarn (dry)
12: Keppel Cove
13: Brown Cove

Rock pinnacle,
Brown Crag

The habit of the west-flowing streams of White Side is interesting. It seems natural that they should feed Thirlmere, but a strip of higher ground alongside the lake turns them north into the outflow, St John's Beck. This perversity of nature has been corrected by the Manchester engineers, who have constructed a water race along the base of the fell to collect the water and divert it south into Thirlmere.

MAP

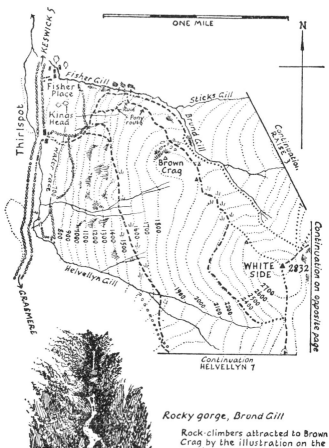

ONE MILE

N

KESWICK 5

Fisher Gill

Fisher Place

Sticks Gill

Kings Head

Thirlspot

Brund Gill

Ruin

Pony route

Continuation RAISE 3

Brown Crag

Helvellyn Gill

WHITE SIDE ▲ 2832

Continuation on opposite page

GRASMERE

800
900
1000
1100
1200
1300
1400
1500
1600
1700
1800
1900
2000
2100
2200
2500
2600
2700

Continuation
HELVELLYN 7

Rocky gorge, Brund Gill

Rock-climbers attracted to Brown Crag by the illustration on the previous page, expecting to see another Napes Needle, will turn away in disgust upon finding it only a few feet high. They may console themselves by trying to climb the nearby gorge in Brund Gill without getting wet.

Waterfalls in Fisher Gill

MAP

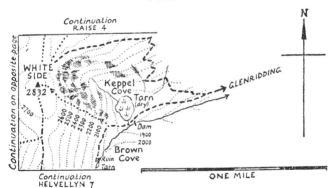

ASCENT FROM THIRLSPOT
2300 feet of ascent : 2½ miles

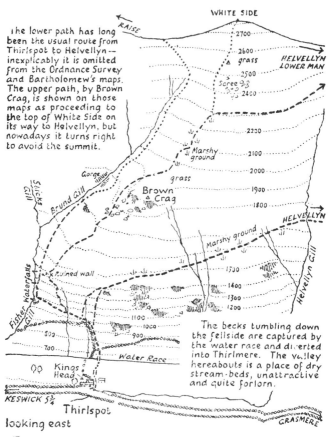

The lower path has long been the usual route from Thirlspot to Helvellyn — inexplicably it is omitted from the Ordnance Survey and Bartholomew's maps. The upper path, by Brown Crag, is shown on those maps as proceeding to the top of White Side on its way to Helvellyn, but nowadays it turns right to avoid the summit.

WHITE SIDE

RAISE

HELVELLYN LOWER MAN

grass

Scree

Marshy ground

Gorge

grass

Brown Crag

Sticks Gill

Brund Gill

HELVELLYN

Marshy ground

Helvellyn Gill

Fisher's Waterfalls

Ruined wall

Fisher Gill

Water Race

Kings Head

KESWICK 5¼

Thirlspot

looking east

GRASMERE

The becks tumbling down the fellside are captured by the water race and diverted into Thirlmere. The valley hereabouts is a place of dry stream-beds, unattractive and quite forlorn.

Two paths cross the western flank of White Side above Thirlspot. They lead to Helvellyn, but the upper one is conveniently placed for the ascent of White Side: it is an easy climb on grass after initial steepness.

ASCENT FROM GLENRIDDING
2400 feet of ascent : 4 miles from Glenridding village

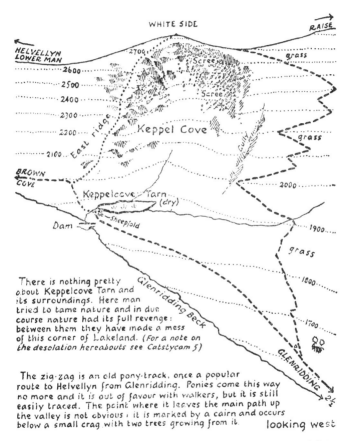

There is nothing pretty about Keppelcove Tarn and its surroundings. Here man tried to tame nature and in due course nature had its full revenge: between them they have made a mess of this corner of Lakeland. *(For a note on the desolation hereabouts see Catstycam 5)*

The zig-zag is an old pony-track, once a popular route to Helvellyn from Glenridding. Ponies come this way no more and it is out of favour with walkers, but it is still easily traced. The point where it leaves the main path up the valley is not obvious: it is marked by a cairn and occurs below a small crag with two trees growing from it.

looking west

There are few high fells more easily climbed than White Side if the zig-zag path from Glenridding is used. The other route shown, by the east ridge, is very different; it is pathless, steep and stony, but not difficult.

THE SUMMIT

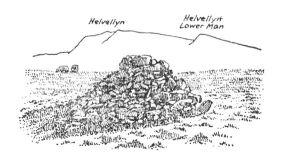

The top of White Side is marked by a large cairn set in a wide expanse of excellent turf, with grassy slopes descending gently on all sides, although north-eastwards the ground falls away sharply around the rim of Keppel Cove.

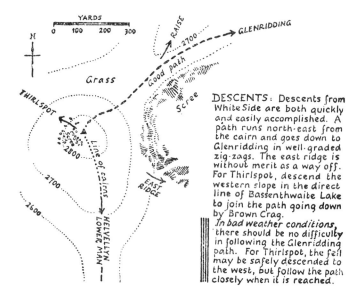

DESCENTS: Descents from White Side are both quickly and easily accomplished. A path runs north-east from the cairn and goes down to Glenridding in well-graded zig-zags. The east ridge is without merit as a way off. For Thirlspot, descend the western slope in the direct line of Bassenthwaite Lake to join the path going down by Brown Crag.

In bad weather conditions, there should be no difficulty in following the Glenridding path. For Thirlspot, the fell may be safely descended to the west, but follow the path closely when it is reached.

THE VIEW

Helvellyn shuts out the distant scene southwards, but in all other directions the panorama is very good, especially to the west. The best picture is provided by Skiddaw, with Bassenthwaite Lake at its foot.

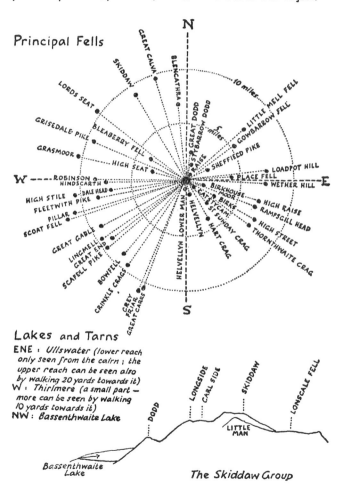

Principal Fells

Lakes and Tarns

ENE : *Ullswater (lower reach only seen from the cairn ; the upper reach can be seen also by walking 20 yards towards it)*
W : *Thirlmere (a small part — more can be seen by walking 10 yards towards it)*
NW : *Bassenthwaite Lake*

The Skiddaw Group

RIDGE ROUTES

To HELVELLYN LOWER MAN, 3033' : 1 mile : S

Depression at 2600'
450 feet of ascent

A grassy descent and a long stony climb.
Easy. Safe in mist.

Follow the line of cairns : a fair path
materialises at the depression and it
continues distinctly up the long ridge
ahead, becoming very loose and stony.

To RAISE, 2889'

¾ mile : NE
Depression at 2650'
250 feet of ascent

Easy walking on grass.
Safe in mist.

A good path leads down to the depression
(and continues down into Glenridding). Strike
up the broad shoulder from the depression —
there is no path — and after reaching a cairn
cross the level plateau to the stony summit.

The ridge south

The East Ridge
*(In the foreground, the burst
banks of Keppelcove Tarn)*

THE EASTERN FELLS
Some Personal Notes
in conclusion

I suppose it might be said, to add impressiveness to the whole thing, that this book has been twenty years in the making, for it is so long, and more, since I first came from a smoky mill-town (forgive me, Blackburn!) and beheld, from Orrest Head, a scene of great loveliness, a fascinating paradise, Lakeland's mountains and trees and water. That was the first time I had looked upon beauty, or imagined it, even. Afterwards I went often, whenever I could, and always my eyes were lifted to the hills. I was to find then, and it has been so ever since, a spiritual and physical satisfaction in climbing mountains — and a tranquil mind upon reaching their summits, as though I had escaped from the disappointments and unkindnesses of life and emerged above them into a new world, a better world.

But that is by the way. In those early Lakeland days I served my apprenticeship faithfully, learning all the time. At first, the hills were frightening, moody giants, and I a timid Gulliver, but very gradually through the years we became acquaintances and much later firm friends.

In due course I came to live within sight of the hills, and I was well content. If I could not be climbing, I was happy to sit idly and dream of them, serenely. Then came a restlessness and the feeling that it was not enough to take their gifts and do nothing in return. I must dedicate something of myself, the best part of me, to them. I started to write about them, and to draw pictures of them. Doing these things, I found they were still giving and I still receiving, for a great pleasure filled me when I was so engaged — I had found a new way of escape to them and from all else less worth while.

Thus it comes about that I have written this book. Not for material gain, welcome though that would be (you see I have not escaped entirely!); not for the benefit of my contemporaries, though if it brings them also to the hills I shall be well pleased; certainly not for posterity, about which I can work up no enthusiasm at all. No, this book has been written, carefully and with infinite patience, for my own pleasure and because it has seemed to bring the hills to my own fireside. If it has merit, it is because the hills have merit.

I started the book determined that everything in it should be perfect, with the consequence that I spent the first six months filling wastepaper baskets. Only then did I accept what I should have known and acknowledged from the start — that nothing created by man is perfect, or can hope to be; and having thus consoled and cheered my hurt conceit I got along like a house on fire. So let me be the first to say it: this book is full of imperfections. But let me dare also to say that (apart from many minor blemishes of which I am already deeply conscious and have no wish to be reminded) it is free from inaccuracies.

The group of fells I have named the Eastern Fells are old favourites, not quite as exciting as the Scafell heights, perhaps, but enjoyable territory for the walker. They are most conveniently climbed from the west, which is a pity, for the finest approaches are from the Patterdale valley to the east. The walking is easy for the most part; very easy along the main watershed. The coves below the summits eastwards are a feature of these hills: rarely visited, they are very impressive in their craggy surroundings. Exploration also reveals many interesting evidences of old and abandoned industries — quarries, mines, aqueducts, disused paths. Somebody should write a geographical history of these enterprises before all records are lost.

Some of my experiences during many solitary wanderings while collecting information for this book would be worth the telling, but I preserve the memories for the time when I can no longer climb. One, however, returns insistently to mind...... I remember a sunny day in the wilderness of Ruthwaite Cove: I lay idly on the warm rocks alongside Hard Tarn, with desolation everywhere but in my heart, where was peace. The air was still; there was no sound, and nothing in view but the shattered confusion of rocks all around. I might have been the last man in a dead world. A tiny splash drew my gaze to the crystal-clear depths of the tarn .... a newt was swimming there, just beneath the surface. I watched it for a long time. And I fell to wondering.......

wondering about it, and its mission as it circled the smooth waters, and the purpose of its life — and mine. A trivial thing to remember, maybe, yet I do. I often think of that small creature, a speck of life in the immensity of desolation in which it had its being.

It is a remarkable thing, now that I come to think of it, that I still set forth for a day on the hills with the eagerness I felt when they were new to me. So it is that I have thoroughly enjoyed my walks whilst this book has been in preparation, much more so because I have walked with a purpose. Yet recently my gaze has been wandering more and more from the path, and away to the fells east of Kirkstone — my next area of exploration.

So, although I take my leave of the Eastern Fells with very real regret, as one parts from good friends, I look forward to equally happy days on the Far Eastern Fells. When this last sentence is written Book One will be finished, and in the same moment Book Two will take its place in my thoughts.

Christmas, 1954   AW.

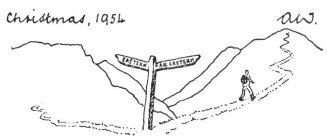